Diary of an Oil Expat Family

Diary of an Oil Expat Family

Heidi Vaughan

Writers Club Press

San Jose New York Lincoln Shanghai

Diary of an Oil Expat Family

Writers Club Press
an imprint of iUniverse.com, Inc.

For information address:
iUniverse.com, Inc.
5220 S 16th, Ste. 200
Lincoln, NE 68512
www.iuniverse.com

Design/Illustration by C. Benjamin Dacus

ISBN: 0-595-18334-4

Printed in the United States of America

For my family

With special thanks to Bethany Bultman, Robin Pascoe, Sondra Fowler, Paul White and Ben Dacus

FOREWORD

So what's an expat?

An expat, short for expatriate, is someone who lives outside one's home country. All kinds of people live in foreign countries for many reasons, though most often it's for a job. Expats can commonly be found in the military, the diplomatic corps, the financial world, technology, those involved with importing and exporting goods and services, and students or other people in special training. The industry with the largest number of employees in foreign locations around the world is the oil business.

So, who should read this book? If you are considering living in a foreign country, for any reason, this book might be helpful. It shows the cycle of culture shock, the unavoidable course of emotions you can expect to go through while living in a foreign land.

You can read a description of culture shock, but this book illustrates very clearly and personally what it's actually all about, what kinds of things bring on stress and irritability in a foreign land, and what really takes place emotionally, during the early months of your assignment. Culture shock is unavoidable, but once you know what to expect, you'll be better equipped to put things in perspective and handle things more successfully.

Just what is culture shock? Culture shock is what occurs when you don't know how to function in your surroundings, when everything is new and nothing is easy, when you can't live your life in a normal way and the stress overwhelms you. The cycle itself lasts about six months, but many people experienced in foreign living say it takes a full year to feel really comfortable in new surroundings.

The initial phase of culture shock starts the day you arrive in your new country. Early on, expats tend to be excited by their new surroundings, viewing everything with an open mind, seeing things as a tourist might. After a few weeks, however, the newness of it all begins to ware off, and some expats may begin to wonder how they will function in the country, which is still really foreign to them. This is when irritability and hostility set in, and problems begin.

Eventually expats get over the hump of culture shock, and things start to get easier. They learn to change and adapt to their surroundings and find ways to be happy where they are. Things seem less foreign, and slowly it even begins to feel like home. Though there may always be good and bad days during the foreign assignment, the worst is over and life becomes balanced and regular again. The cycle of culture shock has run its course.

Saturday morning, February 28, 1998

I'm going to call for a taxi in just a minute, and while I have these few moments left I want to record my thoughts, while I'm having them, because one day in the future I will have forgotten how I feel right now. We're beginning a new chapter in our lives, the four of us, starting today.

The first two of us met in school, married and lived in Chicago. One of us finished graduate school and one of us had a baby. The graduate student, George, started working for Conoco. We settled in Houston with our daughter, Ellen. Then after a few years had a son, Peter. My name is Heidi and I take care of all of them.

And any minute now we are putting ourselves and a lot of our stuff into a taxi to the airport. And very later today, well I guess it will be tomorrow by then, the four of us will begin our new lives in Norway.

We have a huge pile of red duffle bags and I hope we've packed the right stuff for everyone for the next two months or so, while we wait for all our belongings to catch up with us. We are moving ourselves and everything we still own. We sold our house. We sold our cars. We've kept the rest and who knows what will happen but we plan to be gone about five years.

I have been reading everything I can get my hands on about Norway and Scandinavia and I think of that part of the world as a natural wonderland full of mountains, trees, snow and sea. I have never been there. It seems like a magical place for children, with lots of running around in nature and looking for berries and mushrooms and trolls and polar bears, the stuff of fairytales. But what is it really like? I have no idea.

A few months back George was considering taking the job in Norway and I was invited to visit the country with him. I didn't think it would be good to take a baby on that big trip possibly twice in short succession. So I didn't go. I knew I was taking a risk but I value my husband's opinion. George thought Norway was gorgeous, a place for great fishing and sailing, big open spaces to explore, with nice people, a good job, a new way of life to discover. If he thinks this will be a good move for us he's probably right.

Moving abroad is a very big step, though, I know. I have lived abroad once before, in France, when I was a university student. Of course I spoke French. I've looked at a Berlitz book a bit but I really don't know anything about the Norwegian language, except that they have a few extra letters. And unlike last time, I have responsibility. I have a couple of small people I must take care of and help to adjust too, not to mention my husband.

About a year ago we went to a party at the home of a Norwegian friend George knew from work named Christin. There were about 30 people there and we were the only Americans. An odd thing to have happen really, because, well, we were in the United States after all. Everyone else was Norwegian, though. The gathering was friendly and people spoke English with us, and one woman I talked to had just arrived the day before from Norway and she was a bit out of sorts. I had no idea then that we might ever move to Norway. In fact, before that day I hadn't given the country Norway more than one minute's thought in my whole life.

We are going to a town called Stavanger, in the southern part of the country right on the North Sea. Although the country is bisected by the Arctic Circle, Stavanger is hundreds of miles south of it and its supposed to have a mild maritime climate, but with very long days in the summer and very short ones in winter. At the town center is a cathedral which is over 800 years old. Stavanger has been home to various people including those working in the sardine canning industry, and more recently oil, like us. The population is about 100,000, which will make it the smallest town I have ever lived in, but we certainly won't be the only Americans. The town is influenced by the people living there from all around the world, drawn by the oil business. That's what I've read, anyway.

The timing for this change for our family seems to be good and the children are young enough that they should adapt easily. Ellen is four years old and Peter is nine months. I can't work in Norway but I haven't worked for years anyway, so that's one adjustment I won't have to make.

We made what we considered to be a big move three years ago, when we moved to Houston. We found Texas to be, as they say, a whole other country. But after several months we were really feeling settled, we'd begun to have a social life and by a year we got used to the climate. In fact now that we're leaving we're sad about it. We've really enjoyed Houston, we're sad to be leaving friends behind and already we look forward to coming back here to live again some day.

But the hardest part about living way down here in Texas has been being so far from family and friends around Chicago. The distance is going to be the big problem for us in Norway too, we think. The language is something else that concerns us, as does the weather, the darkness, and I am afraid I may be a bit isolated and lonely. They say expat moves are harder on the wife and I wonder how much it helps that I know that. George is starting a new job and I am just sort of ending everything I have, outside the family. I don't look forward to starting over all over again, but I do look forward to new discoveries and I think we've made a good choice.

And just this week George's alumni magazine arrived, one of the last things we got before discontinuing our mail, and the cover story was about the trend towards overseas assignments and living abroad. There was a picture of an American girl on the cover of the magazine who looked quite a lot like our Ellen, wearing a beret, getting into a taxi with her parents, looking a bit sad.

Here we go.

Evening, Sunday, March 1

I've got some nice opera going on the radio and I've just finished unpacking our duffle bags. Seven of them. We got matching red ones because we thought they would be easier to spot and collect at the baggage claim. They were. Hardly anyone has red bags.

Things worked out well. We flew from Chicago to Amsterdam then on to Stavanger. George bumped into someone he knew in Amsterdam and I was so tired I really wasn't very social, which is not like me. Now we're here and everyone is asleep but me.

I feel kind of numb. On the plane I was speaking with a flight attendant from Norway. I told her we were moving here and I asked her to tell me everything about the country. She was shocked when she discovered I was moving here sight unseen, as they say.

Here's one thing I was wrong about: Looking at average temperatures for the coastal town we are in I was under the impression that it would generally be around 50 F most of the year. I thought all the snow was in the mountains or out further from the coast. But in fact it was really snowing when we got in. I couldn't see a thing out the airplane window but snow.

There are about six inches on the ground. And it's kind of unfortunate really that I packed no winter coats or boots, especially for the children. Wait a minute. We moved from Houston. The kids don't even own any snow suits. Plenty of bathing suits though. The thing is we don't have anything appropriate for the weather.

And it is an odd feeling being here. I really don't have a clue what's going on. I can tell you this much, the place is gorgeous. We arrived very early in the morning kind of exhausted and found ourselves in this lovely little airport with so much character. It was just so Scandinavian, very tidy with wooden floors and brightly colored modern furniture and drapes. Unbelievably we stepped up to the police window with our visas and the man behind the counter said, "You must be the Vaughans." Bear in mind I grew up calling O'Hare my home airport.

After customs we were met by an American family, the Eggemeyers, who are here with Conoco and who were kind enough to take us to our apartment. They have two boys, the youngest of whom was Peter's age when they arrived six years ago. Curiously, after six years in Norway they speak no Norwegian.

We had a short but picturesque drive from the airport to the apartment. I've never lived around mountains. Here they provide a lovely view out my kitchen window. We will be here until our furnishings clear customs in several weeks. I was pleased to find that Polly, the wife, had done some shopping for us. The fridge was full of food and there were supplies for cleaning up. I hadn't even thought about that stuff and it was nice not to have to think about it now. She quickly showed me how to use the washing machine and dryer. Odd little machines.

We were grateful for all the Eggemeyers had done for us, but glad when they left us. We needed a moment to just take a deep breath. Polly gave me her number, told me to call with any questions and said she would return the next day to take me shopping. OK.

We needed a look and ventured out for a little walk. All we had were sweaters with fleeces over the top, no boots but hats at least. The apartment is steps from what turned out to be a stunning mirror lake called Mosvatnet, which is settled in a small forest. We walked part of the way around then panicked that we might get lost. We didn't know how long it was around and we were starting to feel cold. But it was beautiful. The snow was perfect. Hardly a footprint and pure white. Lots of ducks and swans were floating about. Everything was calm and quiet.

And we did make an early observation, after just one day. A pretty significant thing, too. While we didn't pass many people, the few we saw didn't look at us, or acknowledge us at all. It was very odd. As Americans we are used to offering some greeting, if not hello then some sort of eye-contact and a smile, tip of head. And as we're used to it, we were doing it. But no one looked at us, just past us. We felt like Crocodile Dundee when he first arrives in New York City and tries to say hello to everybody. We guess we'll have to stop looking at people. So there's one change we'll be making.

Tuesday Morning, March 3

Yesterday was my first day to wake up and go to sleep in Norway. Pleasantly for me, I was unable to write about it last night because we had company.

Christin, the Norwegian woman George worked with in Houston and who also happens to be a native of Stavanger, has since moved back here and stopped by yesterday morning with some warm gear for the kids and a sled. She took George to work then picked me up on her way home last night to take me shopping for clothes. It was such a relief for me because I didn't have to think at all. She showed me what the kids would need: proper snow suits, mittens, hats, boots. The sort of thing I could never have figured out on my own—at least not yet—let alone know where to get things or how much to spend. It turns out Visa may be everywhere you want to be, but it's not in Norway. Not everywhere anyway. They use an ATM cash card everywhere here, and my American one didn't work. So, Christin also paid for all the stuff we bought.

After a drive around she took me to her house to see her family and find some tools. We'd also bought the kids a sled. I've never seen one like this before. It seats two with a steering wheel and a hand brake and it looks like a luge. It's something. I wasn't sure if we had anything with us to put it together and Christine's husband, Marton, took care of it for us.

Their place is really fantastic. It's a huge, sprawling, modern wooden house with lots of original Norwegian art. Windows everywhere take advantage of very wonderful views of Hafrsfjord, the picturesque finger of the North Sea which comes up near their home. After a good look around we all got into the car, Christin, Marton and their daughter Malin, aged three. Their Gordon Setter Gaya also came along.

We drove a short way back to our apartment, and had a nice little hello. At this point we were so excited to be here we were ready to pop. And we had someone to share it with. And even better still, they knew everything.

Earlier in the day I had the chance to see the town a bit. Polly picked me up for a little excursion. We took the kids to a very quaint and terrifically smoky bakery called Skagen Bakeri. I think the building housed the town's first shop, or something like that. In any event, it is very, very old, an historic spot. The walls and floors are tilted and slanted. We all had some open-faced sandwiches, which I understand is a very typical lunch here, and Polly bumped into a few friends. It was nice to see her friends. They seemed nice and I sat imagining myself with friends soon. She also took me to Helgø Matsenter, which I have heard is the nicest grocery store in town.

When I walked in the door the strong smell of fish was a shock, but other than that Helgø's was perfectly fine and I wouldn't complain about anything. It has a lovely bakery section and a very complete fish and meat counter. I ordered some things and forgot I couldn't ask for a half-pound, but needed to say quarter kilo. All the information on the food packages is printed in Norwegian and/or Danish, Swedish and sometimes Finish, but rarely English. I saw all kinds of specialty items the likes of which I used to get at Whole Foods in Houston. I also saw a few things and I wasn't sure what they were. Polly generally knew, and what a huge help for me that she was with me. All in all I was very surprised and impressed at what I could get here. In fact, other than the fishy smell it was quite like a nice grocery store in the United States.

The shopping carts are much smaller than we're used to and I think Norwegians try to shop daily. You also must put a coin into the cart as a deposit. This ensures that you return the cart when you're done shopping. There's nobody there with the job of collecting carts from the small parking lot and you bag your groceries yourself. No high schoolers snapping gum while they ring up your stuff. So some differences but really not so different and not necessarily anything bad.

I spent about $150, thanks to some cash from Polly, and remember I already had food at home. I didn't get much, but it was expensive. Especially beer. A six pack cost $20. Diapers were $10. That's about $3 more than diapers cost in the United States. I assume you know what beer costs.

Also, I realized it was a relief to be with Polly, and I wasn't afraid of talking, speaking English with the lady working at the register. I think if Polly hadn't been there, though, I would not feel so sure of myself or be so comfortable speaking my own language with the locals. Might have actually been scared.

I am a bit nervous about cooking here, too. The ingredients are different and nothing looks exactly like I'm used to it looking. My stove is of course in Celsius. Measurements are different. And I think what people eat here must be very different. I came across some kind of semi-transparent white plastic box full of pale fish balls. I don't think I'll be trying that too soon.

And now I sit again with the radio on. It's actually National Public Radio, way over here in Norway. It's on a few hours a day on the Armed Forces Radio Network. It is a bit of a comfort just now. George and Ellen also are pleased with the television selection at the apartment. Lots of programming is in English including CNN, CNBC, the Cartoon Network and TNT. There's also plenty to see in Norwegian.

Before I left I asked some Norwegians I knew in Houston about kids' television programming, as I was concerned that they would only have some limited selection, all in Norwegian. Their responses were always the same, "Oh, Norwegian children never watch TV."

Evening, Wednesday, March 4

I woke up this morning to the sounds of the radio and a commercial was on which was unlike any I have ever heard before. Here's how it went: "If you want a taste that makes you sing, move your ass to Burger King." Wow. I thought Burger King was so All-American. I don't think we would say "ass" in a radio commercial, would we? Someone might be offended and start a boycott or something. Well, I bounded out of bed with that one. The children, on the other hand, are having a really hard time with their sleep schedules. They have bad jet lag. They are just all messed up and mornings and evenings have been difficult around here. I hope it sorts itself out soon.

I am aware that what I'm going through emotionally now is sort of the honeymoon phase with regards to being in Norway. In a few weeks I'm supposed to get very frustrated, irritated and unhappy but now I'm supposed to be quite content. I am. This tiny washing machine I've got actually holds quite a lot. It takes forever—117 minutes to be exact. It sounds like an airplane landing when it's on its final spin. But it gets clothes super, super clean. I washed one sweater I've had for years and it came out looking like something I'd just bought. The nap on it was totally new again.

And we've been having a lot of fun with the new sled. There's a good little hill right next to the apartment. While we were out a group of children came over from the day care across the street. I had noticed the pile of sleds outside the door and thought it so quaint. About 20 kids came out and it was so nice to watch them enjoy the snow too. One child about Ellen's size was handling himself very well on a pair of skis.

Last night I stayed in to try to get Peter to bed at a decent hour while George and Ellen went sledding on the hill with the radio tower, which, like most every place around here, is lit with electric lights after dark. They went with Christin and Malin. I guess Gaya, their dog, pulled the sled and that was a real thrill for Ellen. They came back with flushed cheeks talking very quickly, animated by their adventurous evening.

My day was quiet. I stayed home with the kids. I still don't have my own car, and I haven't driven here yet anyway. So we've walked around a bit in the neighborhood we're in, on a beautiful street called Eiganesveien, which is lovely. Our place is called Eiganes Terrasse, and it's at the end of the street, which is very long and runs all the way into downtown Stavanger. The houses here are very large, even by Texas standards. I can see pretty drapes in the windows of the houses and many people have plants and lots of orchids in the windows. The houses are a bit older and they have so much character and the streets are so very narrow. I guess you have to pull over to let another car pass, or back up. This place looks like the stuff of storybooks, hardly modern, although already I notice that everyone here carries a mobile phone.

Thursday morning, March 5

I've got all my Norwegian money, called kroner, spread out across a large desk here and I've just finished studying it. I have about $96 on me, more than $10 of which is in coins. Of course I would never normally walk around with that much change, but here the coin denominations are larger. One of the coins is worth nearly $3. I must remember to be careful about that and take more notice of what's falling out of my pockets.

Polly came by again yesterday and took us to see some more things around Stavanger. The shops are all so cute and it is very nice to have Polly to rely on and keep me company. I imagine sometime in the near future I could get a bit lonely. The thing is, you can meet lots of people, but to have a real friend takes some time. For now, I'm glad I have Polly, though she may be ready to get back to her own friends and life soon.

And today while we were out I actually nursed Peter in public. I have never, ever and would never do that in the United States. Nursing in public is just not done much in America and it's not very acceptable socially. I remember once in Houston I was shopping at a nice department store and I asked where I might nurse the baby. They directed me to the ladies bathroom. I opted for a dressing room instead. But here they're doing it anywhere, discreetly, and that's one thing about Norway that's good.

Speaking of babies, the babies here are gorgeous. They all seem to be blond with big blue eyes, wearing beautiful knit sweaters and hats. They are big, too, and they ride around in these fantastic prams with sheepskin linings and silver rattles dangling. A few years ago there was a story about I think a Danish woman who stopped for a drink in New York and left her baby to sleep in the pram outside the restaurant window. It was considered outrageous behavior in New York and I believe she got into some sort of trouble for it. Here the population is tiny, and crime is something I don't think you need to worry about much, and people do in fact leave babies outside sleeping in prams. The temperature seems a bit cold to me but I'm sure the mothers know what they are doing.

And people seem to walk around a lot more here than they do in the United States. Definitely more than Houston. In a place like Chicago, where you do walk a lot if you live in the city, it's quite normal to take a cab at times, especially in bad weather. But here people are walking, despite the weather, just dressed properly with boots and hats and rain gear and even the prams have plastic covers to keep out the snow, and it is not so easy either. The streets are paved with bumpy bricks and the hills can be steep. Of course that makes it so lovely and charming and quaint.

As I walk around I am aware of how very excited I am to be here. Every now and then I notice I have butterflies in my stomach for no reason and I just feel happy and curious to know about everything. The kids don't know anything. Ellen understands we've moved and all that, but she's too young to understand what that really means. We told her we will probably be back living in the United States by the time she is ten, but she can't really conceive of that at her young age. Peter knows he likes familiarity and routine, which he's not got just yet, but we'll be into it soon enough. Everything is just so new, new, new.

Friday, March 6

OK. Last night we experienced the Norwegian Vinmonopolet, the state-run liquor and wine monopoly. You can buy beer at the grocery store. Everything else comes from the Vinmonopolet. We shuffled back and forth between two very small display cases before we realized that's what they were: very small displays. We noticed amongst the considerable crowd standing in numerous long lines, that everyone was looking at these small books, about the size of a playbill from a show.

Inside was listed, in Norwegian, of course, what was available. There were short descriptions (if only we could have read them) and prices. I guess you look at the book, pick what you want then order at the counter. You never get to actually look at anything besides the words in the book. The lines were so long I felt like I was in Russia and the prices were crazy. Hard liquor was anywhere from $40 to $60 per bottle. Wine was more reasonable, but there were no cheap bottles.

Amongst our purchases was a Mouton Cadet cabernet I used to buy at the grocery store in Houston. It cost about $10, maybe a dollar or more beyond what I was used to paying back home. There really wasn't anything cheaper than that. Few things cost much more either. Well, a few. There were mainly French, Italian, German and Australian wines. A few Californian. We were told they don't always have everything listed in stock, so it's good to have some alternatives in mind by the time it's your turn.

The hours of operation at the Vinmonopolet are 10 to 6, I think, on the weekdays, and until 2:00 p.m. Saturdays. Thursday is special, when they are open until 7:00 p.m. All in all a bit inconvenient, but I heard there is an effort made so that nobody can buy alcoholic beverages during a time they are likely to consume them. In the United States of course if you run out during a party you can send someone to get more. That can never happen here.

Incidentally, those hours are also the hours of most of the shops, at least in the center of town. There are a couple of malls around, which are open until 8:00 p.m. on a weekday. Nothing is open on Sunday. That is a change for us.

And I'm finding people don't all speak English so well. I'm pretty sure some people have said yes, shook their heads yes, but inside it was more "whatever." I went into a drug store, called an Apotek, and asked for some diaper cream. The woman working there didn't know what I meant by "diaper rash." I looked in my English/Norwegian dictionary and couldn't find it. So I said "baby red" and pointed to my backside. She did emerge with a tube of something and I think she understood…

Let me tell you about the pharmacy, because it was nice and it happens to be next door to the Vinmonopolet. I always like going into pharmacies when I travel because they have neat new things I want to try. Well in Norway, if you have a prescription, you take a number and wait. When it's your turn you get to sit down in a nice comfortable chair at your own private area for a consultation. Everyone seems happy and calm. If you've ever been to the pharmacy at Walgreen's and waited in a giant, hectic crowd with a sick, screaming child in your arms, well, this is the opposite of that.

The snow has mostly melted with rain and warmer weather. Marton told me it rains 200 or 220 days out of the year here, something like that. It sounds like an awful lot, doesn't it? Two days of precipitation for every dry one. What I discovered under the snow though were huge rocks and boulders, green grass and everything all covered with lots of green moss, even on the trees. With all the moss and blowing mist I can now understand how close we are to Scotland. And I've seen zillions of what look like perhaps crocuses coming up. Tulips seem to be getting started. Rhododendrons are everywhere and all budded up. Spring seems to have begun here and we're glad because we are used to a hot climate and we've been freezing lately.

Of course there are no leaves on the trees yet and the way the trees are trimmed really confuses me. Many trees are topped. By my understanding that means they are ruined forever. Their natural shape is gone for good. I always detested the was some crepe myrtles are butchered in Houston. What's going on here is far worse. Some of the trees look like something you'd see in a large-bird exhibit at the zoo, like an eagle roost or something. There is a stand of trees on the edge of downtown that is so knobby and misshapen from over pruning it looks like something conceived by a crazy Norwegian artist.

And speaking of strange things, George has been acting very strange. I hope he likes his new job. I have been to his office, which is very, very nice. It's on a fjord, with beautiful views of the water and boats. Big ships and the ferry to Newcastle pass by, and it's very industrial but still nice. There is a big dock next to Conoco full of sailboats and some powerboats. Inside the building it's open and modern with beautiful colorful furniture and wood floors almost red in color. There's a quaint area for coffee, tea, cappuccino, espresso, and there are newspapers around and it seems like a very good place to relax or catch up with someone. The people there have been friendly to me too.

Evening, Saturday, March 7

It's Saturday night around 9:00 p.m., or 21:00 as the time is officially referred to here. Thanks to Christin I now understand what the numbers are which I see on the sides of plenty of the buildings around. They'll just say Rimi, 9-20 (18). What that means is the grocery store, called Rimi, is open from 9:00 a.m. until 8:00 p.m. (and 6:00 p.m. on Saturdays). Speaking of Christin, we had dinner last night with her and Marton at their house, along with another Norwegian family who has lived in Houston. The husband's name is Trond-Erik and the wife is Hilde. The children's names are Kyrre and Gaute. Do you have any idea how to pronounce their names? Well neither do I. They are boys, by the way.

When I was in school I remember reading Dostoyevski and having trouble getting into it because I couldn't keep track of who was who because the names just didn't fit into any context I could understand. It was like that last night. I know I still haven't gotten Malin's name pronounced right either. I think it's something like MAH lean.

So anyway we were there and it was nice to be invited out. And it was nothing to fear. Everyone was very friendly and the food was Italian. We're a bit afraid we're going to be served something very local that we don't like. It's bound to happen sometime. One time I remember being served some cold fish with a kind of jelly on top at the home of a Finnish family. Something like that is coming surely.

I had read somewhere that it is customary to bring flowers when you visit a Norwegian person's home, and we did. Trond-Erik and Hilde did too, so there must be something to that. Here's something important to know about Norway, too. It is illegal to drink alcohol and drive a car. Well, it is in the United States, too, isn't it? But it's different here. They regularly have police checks set up at various points I guess and it's not unusual to be stopped.

You can have 0.05 per cent alcohol in your blood, which I read is equivalent to a light beer or half a glass of wine. Here's why you wouldn't want to drink anything at all, though. If you are stopped by the police you breathe into a Breathalyzer and if any alcohol is detected you immediately lose your license and are taken to the emergency room to have blood drawn. Your license is kept with the police until the results are in, which could take a month! So at the best you are very, very inconvenienced and embarrassed. If it turns out you are over the legal limit you are fined. The amount of the fine is determined by your past year's tax statement. They take one month's income. On top of that you lose your license and go to jail. Is it any surprise to hear that no one here drinks anything and then drives?

There is a further side to it too. Not only does no one drink and drive, it would be considered shameful and irresponsible and selfish if you did. It's sort of the way smoking has become in the United States. You are very, very bad and selfish if you do it, and not only will you die from it, you also go to hell. Incidentally, none of that smoking regulation stuff seems to have caught on here yet. People smoke everywhere and a lot. But back to the drinking and driving, get this: Sixty per cent of the people who are caught driving with alcohol in their systems are stopped not the night of the dinner or the party, but the next day, in the morning on their way to work or or church or wherever. It's so 1984.

I should mention that I have a number of books about Norway, and I've looked at some websites, but the most valuable source of information I have is a book I got from Conoco. It's called "SPINning Around Stavanger," and it is put out by a group of oil companies under the name of Stavanger Partner Information Network. I don't know if books like these are available in the Middle East, the Far East, or all the other places oil expats end up, but they should be. What a terrific resource with lots of local information, useful words, maps, lists of events, organizations. Everything.

And now before I close let me say that it really was a pleasure being out last night and we really enjoyed the company. So far the only Norwegians we've met have lived in the United States and really like Americans, and we appreciate that. I was also a bit worried I would get here and have nothing to do. I was so busy getting everything planned and organized to move here. It was so hectic and I remember showing my good friend Margaret in Houston my calendar for February and it was so full with stuff I had to do we had a good laugh just looking at it. Then I turned the page and showed her March. Nothing at all. Not one thing. But I've been kept plenty busy and I'm feeling pretty good about our prospects for being happy while we're here.

Morning, March 9

We've been in Norway a week. Yesterday was my first time to drive a car here. I wanted to practice for tonight, when I will drive to my first Norwegian language lesson by myself.

So here's what you need to know about driving in Norway: You drive on the right side of the road, same as any other country never under British rule. Roads are marked with either a yellow diamond or no yellow diamond. If you are on a yellow- diamond road you have the right-of-way over cars approaching from side streets. If it is not a yellow-diamond road any car approaching from a street on your right has the right of way. This is sort of in place of a stop sign I think, and it will take some getting used to.

In heavy-traffic intersections, instead of a light you have a roundabout. It's a big rotary where right-of-way is given to cars already in the roundabout or which are approaching from the left. There's not too much traffic and it's a system that runs efficiently. It's a bit scary at first though. I think the trick is once you commit to going into the roundabout, stick with it and don't stop. Nothing else is really different except the speeds are lower than I'm used to. Drivers are courteous and I have not heard one car horn beep since I've been in town. A real change from my years living in downtown Chicago and driving the horrendous Katy Freeway, but it's a much, much smaller town, now, isn't it.

We have all learned a few Norwegian words and we are using them whenever we go out. They are "hei" for hello, "ha det" for goodbye and "tusen takk" for thank you very much. Ellen used the latter recently and the store clerk was so impressed she gave Ellen a piece of candy. Now that's positive reinforcement. I really think it would have made things easier, though, if we had had a formal primer on Norway, and some language lessons before we got here.

And just a few negatives. First of all, I don't like the way kids dress here, and by kids I mean teenagers. I think perhaps they have been spending too much time watching MTV, and more specifically, the Spice Girls. Here's the outfit: Very, very low-slung hip-hugger pants, in polyester or some other man-made fabric, but with huge, huge bell bottoms that pool over gigantic platform lace-up gym shoes, usually black. Then on top is some sort of micro-fiber-ish tummy-show-er t-shirt with cap sleeves—so sad because it all really is flattering to so few—then for a coat some super long thing that nearly trails the ground, sometimes even trimmed in feathers, and the total effect is like something from the Creature Cantina. Thankfully people don't wear much make-up here. Otherwise the look would be even more ridiculous. I think I'll stop being critical of all the American kids I see uniformed in the Gap. It's just fine with me.

The other thing I don't like to see is the graffiti. It is everywhere, and really such a shame to see on the quaint old buildings and in the midst of the beautiful natural surroundings. I have asked a few Norwegians about it, and they say, "Oh, it's just street art." OK, well, I'm from Chicago and I view graffiti differently. It's about turf battles in violent areas under gang domination, a sign of drugs, poverty and other bad things, a warning to avoid this area. Looking around I can't see any sign of gang activity other than the graffiti, nobody that looks like a gang banger, or any need for it. Everyone here is taken care of. Nobody is poor, on drugs, uneducated. Not that I see, anyway.

But in the parking garage on the harbor, a few doors down from Skagen Bakeri, the stair wells are loaded with graffiti and I found myself clutching my purse to my side, turning my diamond rings around and holding my fists tight, checking over my shoulder. This is my natural reaction to seeing this much violent graffiti in one place after living on the Near North

Side of Chicago, on the edge of Cabrini Green, one of America's most dangerous housing projects, for seven years. If I saw this parking garage in Chicago I wouldn't go in it.

In France I remember seeing graffiti of things like Tweety and thinking, Wow, they must not have too much to rage against here. I feel the same way about Norway except that the graffiti is violent, incorporating the themes of the real American gang bangers, with crowns and stars and blue and red. I think it's really sad to see it here and it really has no place here either. What Norwegian kids must not realize is that this kind of graffiti actually means something, and what it means is not good.

Oh, and one more thing. When George Bush was president of the United States he enacted something called the Citizens with Disabilities Act, and what it did was ensure that public places would be handicapped-accessible. I'm not sure if that's the extent of the act, but that's what I know of it and I think it has been a good thing. I've never pushed a wheelchair, but I have had two children in strollers, which need the same kind of access as a wheelchair would. In the United States you can travel around fairly easily, getting into shops or the places you want without too much difficulty. But here they don't have any of that and I find it can be very tricky getting around with a stroller. Which really surprises me because so many people are pushing them around town.

Wednesday, March 11

The highpoint of the day was going with our housing contact at Conoco to look at the houses that are available to us. I didn't think we'd get to do it so soon and I was pleased that the whole process was quite enjoyable. We were informed that we would be shown three houses and that we should try to choose one of them, but other expats had told me we could see more if we demanded it. I just got here and I don't want to demand anything, where would I get off? Anyway we are not very demanding people. I do think there are some people who do their best to sort of maximize the system, though. More experienced expats, no doubt. Some people I've met have been doing this expat thing for years, in fact.

It was raining, something we're getting very used to, and we were asked to leave our shoes at the door when we walked into the homes. We have figured out that Norwegians don't wear shoes in the house like we do. This is a change for us, but given the wet weather and need for boots here, it does make some sense.

We were shown one house that was within walking distance of Conoco, which is located in that industrial area right on the sea. Though walking to work would be a plus we were not too excited about the industrial aspect of the area. The house was super, though. We would have been the first people to live in it; it was brand new and very large.

The second house we saw was in a terrific location, on a street called Gustav Vigelandsveien, a few houses down from a sheep farm and on a lake called Stokkavatnet. It would have been fine for us but it was in need of a bit of redecorating, especially in the kitchen. The wallpapers were drab and old, the light fixtures were kind of scary, and the house was dark, but very fixable.

In the end the third house was also on the lake, which incidentally translates to "the Stokka lake." Only this house was up on a hill so it had terrific views of the water, and a very nice garden, a huge, open floor plan, and it was modernized. Though it appeared smallish from the outside, it wasn't. And inside it reminded us of a giant ski lodge. It's in a neighborhood called Sandal, on a street called Sandal Terrasse, quite an easy street name as they go around here. Needless to say the third is the house we picked.

Norwegian homes are quite unlike American ones, and there is little variation between them. First, they are nearly always wooden. Usually they are painted white, yellow, brown or dark red. They have tile roofs, usually the typical orange clay or sometimes a glazed tile, often in royal blue. Occasionally, if it's an older home, the roof is slate. My favorite though, is the roof you will see covered in grass and other growing things. I passed one with a goat up on the roof eating it.

Houses tend to look smaller from the outside than they are, unlike in Houston where you might find a grand entrance and little behind it. Here they sometimes look small, but they are huge. Ours has three stories and five bedrooms, maybe about 4,000 square feet in total. I don't think it's atypical, though many people would perhaps rent the bottom floor, which is often partially underground, as an apartment.

Many Norwegian floors are heated, especially in the bathrooms but also throughout the house, which often will have all wooden flooring. Walls and even ceilings are frequently paneled in bare pine. I've noticed fewer windows than we tend to have in the United States, and unless the house is really modern, the windows are almost always square, with no dividers of any kind. Garages are not as common as carports, and driveways are not always paved. The gardens in general are less formal than ours in the United States are, and weeds don't seem to annoy people to the extent they do back home. In all, the outdoor spaces are more natural, often without fencing, and well cared for.

And here's the best part, to me anyway: After every few houses you'll find a playground, called a "lekeplass." I counted six in my new neighborhood, and I don't know if I saw them all. Christin told me that kids Ellen's age are allowed to walk alone to these playgrounds, and that they can play safely by themselves, but usually lots of kids are there. I also read that cars should drive at walking pace when in residential areas, and that children have the right of way in the road.

By contrast, in my neighborhood in Houston I would have to say it was the youngest drivers who had the right of way in the streets, and by that I mean the 16 year olds in cars, not kids on bikes. Little children in our neighborhood liked to play on riding toys on the driveway and I often would run into the street after a car whizzed by and yell, "slow down!"

In Norway you must be 18 to get your drivers license, by the way. You must take driving lessons and have a big L posted on your car for a year to let people know you are learning. Young people can get a driver's license for motorcycles when they are only 16, so you do see a fair amount of kids driving those. By the time kids are 18 though they are more mature and safer, I believe. It's a better age to begin to drive.

So we've got a house, and we will move in after our furniture finishes its trip across the ocean and clears customs. We can't wait.

Morning, Sunday, March 15

Last night we went to a Texas party at the Radisson SAS Royal hotel. Entertainment included the Phillips Singing 66 Choir and, believe it or not, a square-dancing demonstration by a local group called the Stavanger Squares. I thought it was really odd that people in Norway would square dance. Even though I'm American, I've never even known anyone who could square dance. Or anyone who would want to. But here these Norwegians even had the outfits. George joked that it would balance the people in the United States who might be sitting home knitting a Norwegian sweater.

We met the new Ambassador to Norway at the party, a man named David Hermelin, from Michigan. My best friend Kirste had mentioned when I told her we were moving here that she knew the Norwegian ambassador. She had gone to school with his daughter. So while George and I were talking to the Ambassador, we mentioned Kirste. Sure enough he lit up at the mention of my best friend's name. Can I say it? Is this a small world or what?

And now let me change subjects a bit and write for a moment about the standard of living. I'm used to living in a society with a huge range of wealth and varying income and education levels. Suddenly I've stepped into a society that isn't like that at all; at least it doesn't seem like it to me in the short time I've been here. I've not seen one homeless person or banged up car. All the houses are nice. Nobody is dressed in poor clothes, questionable fashions, yes, but not poor. I'm not sure if it's because I'm in a small town (I haven't been to Oslo yet, but I do live in one of the larger cities, the fourth largest in fact), or if it is entirely due to the fact that this is a very socialist society, but everyone looks to be doing well.

It is awfully nice to only be exposed to people who are clean, nice-smelling, educated and well dressed. Somehow it just doesn't seem very realistic to me, though. It seems too good to be true.

It's also strange to see such homogeneity. There are few non-Norwegians here, at least by my American-melting-pot standards. We've met some African Americans here with Conoco. They must feel like they really stand out. Our kids have blond hair and blue eyes. This makes it easy for them but I wonder what it's like for children who look very different.

Wednesday, March 18

Today was a quiet day and we actually needed it, we just haven't slowed down since we got here. I'm not seeing so much of Polly but now a very nice Conoco wife named Carolyn is helping me out and she's shown me some other things, like antique shops and other less essential stuff.

Since I have no news for today, let me tell you about last Sunday. We had plans to see a beach nearby. There are in fact lots and lots of beaches nearby, as we live on the coast and Norway has a very long coast like California. Probably there aren't too many other similarities between here and there though. As it was we were heading out with our very best friend Christin, and Malin and the dog. Marton was away on business in the United States, and he often is. Our first stop was a little beach on Hafrsfjord, about 30 steps from the door of Christin's house.

Before I tell you about the beach, I should tell you a little something about Hafrsfjord first. It is a fjord, which is a little piece of the sea that has made it's way inland. It looks more like a lake, because of the shape of it, you can see across it, but it is salt water. Where Christin's house is happens to be very near the sight of a famous Viking battle, in which Harald Hårfagre (the fair-haired) emerged victorious and was named king of all Norway, in about 1075. Prior to that Norway was made up of many small kingdoms. The event is commemorated by "The Three Swords," three towering Viking swords each maybe 40 feet tall sunk into the rocks along Hafrsfjord. It was the first sight I saw when I got to Stavanger, as we passed it coming from the airport. It is huge and the effect is excellent. Ellen is sure they have giants in Norway, otherwise how else could those big swords get there?

Anyway, we stopped first at the little beach on Hafrsfjord. Christin's neighbors have a very neat old wooden boat docked there. It's an old fishing boat, I think. They use it to collect crabs and of course to fish. The water is very deep and very cold. In the summer the kids swim in the fjord, though it never gets warm, and I imagine they have quite a blast.

Looking down off the pier the water was crystal clear. We could see a huge starfish that must have been more than 20 feet down. There were lots of small fish and jellyfish. I've never lived by the sea before so it's all very exciting and new to me.

Driving about 15 minutes along the coast from there we came to the beach at Ølberg. There is an expression in Norway, Norwegians walk on Sunday. As few shops or businesses are open on Sunday there's not much to do beyond church, museums and eating out, except to be active in the outdoors. The weather looked very shaggy to me but there were plenty of people out walking on the beach. Actually, the weather was too bad for us. It was raining, again, and though Norwegians don't seem to mind rain, we do. We felt cold and clammy so we went to the food stand on the beach and ordered some burgers and fries.

The food was so hot and that made us feel better as we sat out in the rain eating it. The fries were very, very greasy, and they came with a little fork. I guess Norwegians don't use their hands as much as we do to eat. The forks are something special for the fries. Burgers and sandwiches are usually eaten with a knife and fork, I think too. Our hamburgers were very unusual. First of all, they were topped with a pinkish sauce that was kind of sweet. On top also was cabbage and corn, amongst the more common burger toppings. The whole number was very large and flat, like a giant plate, and I don't know if it was the proximity to the sea or what, but it tasted like fish, really. The meal was such a heavy load on my stomach I never got hungry again the rest of the day.

The weather showed no signs of improvement so we moved on. Next to Stavanger is a town called Sandnes, population about 50,000, and some people I have met live there. The town looks newer to me than Stavanger maybe, not quite as quaint with more modern buildings and a very modern-looking shopping street, called Langgata. From there we headed over to a farm owned by Christin's father-in-law, who was quite a character.

We had not called first, so we weren't expected. But that was no problem at all. Christin's father-in-law was very welcoming and friendly and he was very good about showing kids things they would find interesting. We met a retired racehorse named Rebecca's Boy, real sheep dogs—border collies, which looked just like the ones in "Babe"—and we saw lots of sheep. One big old male called Oskar let Christin's father-in-law ride him. That was something, as was the whole visit to a Norwegian farm, to our urban family.

The few days since then I've spent meeting new people. The Conoco wives are a very friendly group who work very hard to help you feel welcome and settled. Yesterday I had lunch at a woman named Jackie's house. She was kind to invite other wives over to meet me for lunch and it was very enjoyable. It is interesting to get different perspectives on how to successfully live as an American in a foreign country. Plus the wives know everything. The names of foods I'm looking for, where to buy this or that. It is a bit of a drain being new though, always having to be "on," making niceties, smiling, smiling, smiling.

Though I say I am busy, we really are spending a lot of quiet time together, the kids and me. Peter naps twice a day and goes to bed early, so we are in fact home quite a bit. It seems like I'm always whispering, "don't wake the baby," around the apartment.

We have made good use of the lake near us, too, Mosvatnet, which we visited the first day and which is a walk across the street from our apartment. Our air shipment came a few days ago so now Ellen has her bike and we have more toys. We spend some time every day walking around the lake and playing at the playground. It's very nice and we're going at a much slower pace for now than we did in Houston.

By Mosvatnet is a fantastic museum that I really should mention. I visited it by myself one of the first days I arrived and I have stopped in since for a quick look, coffee and cakes with the kids. It's called the Rogaland Kunstmuseum. Rogaland is the name of the county we live in and "Kunstmuseum" means art museum. It is in fact a lovely sampling of Norwegian art housed in a very modern, very fascinating building. On my first visit I saw an exhibition of the French artist Jean Dubuffet's work. It was featured in the half of the museum dedicated to traveling exhibitions. On the other side is a permanent collection that displays Norwegian art, which I would have to characterize as mostly dark looking, bleak representations of people and life. Hope there's no foreshadowing there for me. No, really there are also lovely landscapes and when I look at them I can already recognize Norway in them.

A café is in the front of the museum, inside a huge solarium that makes you feel as if you are actually sitting outside looking at the lake and the people passing by, but without being bothered by the elements. Have I mentioned that we can't seem to get warm since we got to Norway? It always seems to be raining or sleeting or snowing or all three at the same time.

I am doing a better job of getting around though. Driving is not difficult but that yield-to-cars-approaching-from-the-right thing is hard to remember. It's also really hard to get to people's homes. Nobody seems to know street names, so they say things like: "Then turn right at the yellow house." "I know it doesn't look like a street but it really is one." "Be sure not to drive on the sidewalk, it looks just like a road." And I stall the car constantly, as I'm not used to driving a stick shift or driving on steep hills.

But today I made it to two places by myself, the green grocers (aha, that's where all the nice lettuce is) and Obs!, sort of a Norwegian Target. I also toured Ellen's new preschool which she begins on Monday, called The Children's House. It's in a town called Sola, between Stavanger and

Sandnes. When I called for directions I was told the turn was right after a big strawberry farm. "Oh yes," I said, "I saw that strawberry farm last week when I got lost looking for something else. I know exactly where it is."

Afternoon, Sunday March 22

It's actually warm out in the sun, if you're protected from the wind. I'm sitting outside on our little balcony wearing fairly light clothes and feeling very, very happy. I feel like I'm on a ski vacation in Colorado or Vermont or someplace like that. The sun is shining, the snow is bright and lots of people are out and about. It seems like every day that we've been here there has been some precipitation. We really haven't seen the sun for three weeks and I'm definitely appreciating it today.

Yesterday was probably my roughest day here. Nothing bad happened but I was in a low mood, probably a culmination of all the times I've gotten lost and been unable to find what I need. I grumped around most of the day and then made a few phone calls to the United States in the evening. That made me feel infinitely better.

We have been having fun lately. I got together for coffee and a playgroup with some very nice English-speaking people last Friday, at the home of a Conoco wife named Chrissa. I got to meet more people and the kids enjoyed themselves. That night Christin and her family came to the apartment for dinner and George and I actually had the opportunity to both drink alcohol on the same occasion (remember that designated-driver thing?) and it was nice and relaxing.

I am troubled a bit with Peter. He still isn't settled and he's just not himself and I decided I should take him to the doctor. Before we left the United States we all had very comprehensive physicals and Peter was found to be anemic and he has since been taking iron. My pediatrician in Houston told me to be sure to follow up with it in Norway, so I asked the wives where to take him and I made an appointment.

In general I feel like health care and the health-care process in the United States is very good. I briefly belonged to an HMO. I thought that was pretty awful, but other than that, in general I have always felt satisfied. I've also been pleased with the care my children have gotten from pediatricians. But moving or even just traveling to a foreign country can bring worries about health care, and I've had them.

I remember calling my mother from France after the one time I went to the doctor there.

"Well what did the doctor say?"

"He said I have bronchitis."

"Did he give you anything?"

"Yes, something called Demerol."

"Good Lord, Heidi. You don't need Demerol. That's strong, addictive stuff. I took that when I was in labor with you."

"Well, it really is working. I feel much better."

"I bet you do."

The weird thing about that doctor's appointment was that I spent the whole time standing there completely nude.

And likewise everything about our trip to the Norwegian pediatrician was different. First of all, you can only call the doctor between 10:30 a.m. and noon. For the childless, in the United States your pediatrician or one of his or her partners is on-call 24-hours-a-day. At first I kept getting a busy signal. When the nurse finally answered the phone, I felt like the lucky radio call-in winner. She was nice, though, and I was able to get in the next day. I was totally confused by the directions so George asked a Norwegian friend from work to call the nurse back and get directions then explain them to us. That was a good idea.

We met the doctor, and he seemed very nice and genuinely listened to what I said. Then the nurse drew some of Peter's blood. I couldn't believe that she didn't wear any gloves. Is there really a place in the world where people aren't afraid of AIDS? Anyway, the doctor said things look fine with Peter and he took a look at Ellen too, since she was there. He just picked her up and plopped her on his desk. He talked to her kindly, asked her some questions and looked her over. Ellen has a real fear of doctors but she was relaxed and calm this time.

The doctor explained to us what we could do in the future with the children and their healthcare. First is something called the Health Station. It's run by the Kommune, in our case the Stavanger Kommune, as they call the local but very important governments here. You don't go there when you are sick, just for regular check ups and immunizations. Then there is the Legevakt, that's a place like an emergency room but it's not for emergencies, just acute illness. Or you can go to a private doctor, which is what I am used to doing in the United States, and I will just stick with that I think.

I felt funny just walking out the door when the appointment was over. But it turns out healthcare for all people under age seven in Norway is totally free.

Evening, Tuesday, March 24

Today I had a really bad day.

I had stopped into Obs! (Funny name, isn't it? I consulted the dictionary and the word means "look, notice." This is the place that's kind of like the American Target.) I went in to pick up a few things, especially wool underwear, we're all just freezing, and I decided to drive directly from the store to Ellen's school. Up until now every time I go someplace I always drive by the apartment first, because I know how to get places from there. It's a stupid way to get by and I decided that since I had 45 minutes to get to school I had plenty of time to try going a new way.

So I began to drive a new route and Peter was snoring away in the back seat as I got more and more lost. I couldn't find the main road I needed, though I turned at the sign for it. All the while I was driving the signs on the road said the number of the main road I was looking for. It didn't look familiar, though. The rain was coming down so hard I couldn't even hear the radio. The wind was buffeting the car all over. These gigantic trucks, worlds bigger than any truck I've seen before, kept flying past me, blinding me with the rain the wheels brought up and nearly running me off the road. They all said in great big letters across the front STANGELAND. To me it looked like it said STRANGE LAND.

I became really lost, hopelessly lost. Then I started to stress out. First I started talking to myself out loud about what a fool I was to move to this country and then I started to cry. Finally I saw a gas station and pulled in. Two young men were working there and they both looked up when I came in, concerned when they saw me crying, and I asked them if they spoke English and one of them said yes, a bit. I told them that I'd gotten lost looking for my daughter's school, that it got out in five minutes and that I had no idea where it was or where I was. I asked if he could find the number, call the school, tell them I would be late then find out how I could get there from where I was.

He said yes. And he did all that for me. I was so incredibly grateful, lucky that I had chanced on such a sympathetic person. I had driven around crazily in really heavy rain for a long time. I was a wreck. But things weren't really that bad and in about 10 minutes I was at the school, reunited with my child, who had no clue anything was wrong. Despite my incessant shouting of swear words while driving Peter was in fact still sleeping too. But I was shaking as I told the teacher my tale, and she listened very kindly. In the end she told me I was just being Swedish.

I think I mentioned that Ellen started at a new school on Monday. It's called The Children's House, and it is a preschool specializing in English-language education, though it does offer one class all in Norwegian for children wishing to learn the language. Ellen is enrolled in that class and she has two teachers, Siri, a Norwegian woman, and Ms. Caroline, a Scottish woman who has lived in Norway since the 1970s.

We have a real desire for the whole family to learn to speak Norwegian, for many reasons. First, we live in Norway. That's the most important one. We live here. The thing is we moved to Norway to experience another way of living. It is possible to live here and never learn the language, we have seen that. The thing is, if you never mix with the people in the country, if you don't adapt anything from it into your own life, try the food, visit the sites, understand a bit of their politics, whatever it is, it's not really like living there.

With this in mind we are trying out the Norwegian class at this school. I did visit the day care across the street from the apartment, called Huskestua, which looks very nice, would offer total immersion, but they were full. We joined their association in the event anything opens up. Ellen is young enough for full immersion without the stress an adult would experience, we believe.

And you know, we have been amazed watching children here in Norway. They are very different from American children. First of all they wear an awful lot of protective clothing, for warmth and to stay dry. Then they play outside, everyday, in all weather. They even play at the playground in heavy rain, really. I have learned another expression the Norwegians have: There's no bad weather, just bad clothes. Well there's one way to look at it anyway. Norwegian children also are dangerous daredevils. I always see them in trees, on rooftops, balancing atop tall fences. They are perhaps a bit undisciplined. They seem very healthy and happy too.

There is a branch of the government here called the Ministry of Children and its job is to protect the rights of children. It is against the law to spank a child in Norway. I understand children are given a document listing their rights, which is explained to them, and they are encouraged to post the document somewhere their parents will regularly see it. And the government gives all pregnant women about $5,000, just before they deliver, so they can buy everything they need for a new baby. All parents receive about $160 per month, per child, called milk money; to purchase items the children need, like clothing, toys and shoes.

Is this some kind of country or what? All that running wild in nature, no spanking, free money. It certainly seems like a great place to be if you are a kid.

Morning, Thursday, March 26

Um. I'm feeling a bit delicate this morning. I was out last night for a drink and dinner with the Conoco wives. Perhaps I overdid it slightly. The dinner was arranged by Chrissa, whom I met a week ago. She is a trained chef from New Orleans and a real expert on anything food- or drink-related in Norway, or anywhere I think. Once a month she arranges a night out at a restaurant for the ladies. We stopped first in the bar of a restaurant called Harry Peppers for what Chrissa said was the Best Margarita in Town. It was a tiny drink, served in a juice glass rimmed with table salt.

Then we were on to a very lovely French restaurant called Jans, which I expect might be the nicest place in town. It was definitely on par with the nicest French restaurants I've been to, and I've been to some very nice ones.

When we arrived we were greeted at the door by the owner Jan. He apparently is a friend of Chrissa's; both share a common interest in food, wine and golf. He told us about what we would be eating, served course after course, and checked in with us frequently to see if we were happy. We ate absolutely delicious and beautiful food for three-and-a-half hours, and the evening was truly special.

As I knew I would be drinking (I was right there), I decided to try taking the bus to the restaurant. Though I am an old public transportation pro from living in Chicago, I was a bit worried. Public transportation can take a while to get the hang of anywhere, but especially so if you don't speak the language. I live near a very main road. The main road into town, in fact. So I went to the stop and waited. Incidentally it costs about $2.50 to ride the bus. The ride was about 10 minutes.

Another woman walked up to the stop and I asked her if she could speak English. She did and I asked her for advice on getting to town. She was very nice and very helpful, and when the bus came she sat down next to me and we talked some more. She asked what I thought of Norway and told me she had been an au pair in the United States a few years ago. She had traveled all over America and she obviously liked Americans. And why shouldn't she?

Thursday, April 2

On Sunday we were here a month. We celebrated nicely with a ski getaway in the mountains. We stayed at a place called Sinnes Fjellstue in an area called Sirdal, which is about an hour and a half from Stavanger. The trip was arranged by Conoco, and everyone who was staying at the hotel was with the company.

We enjoyed everything about the weekend, especially the drive up there. We hadn't been out into the mountains yet, and we couldn't believe how incredibly beautiful they were. George and I started the drive by practicing along with our Norwegian language tapes in the car, but we were so overcome by the intense beauty of our surroundings we just had to stop the tapes so we could oooh aaaah.

The granite rock here is very dark and climbs up straight from the highway, which twists, turns, and goes up and down, through tunnels bored through the mountains. There are few plants but water is dripping down, down, down from all around. Waterfalls are everywhere, with water falling from so high above us it was incredibly, absolutely fantastic to behold. To the side of the road white waters raged in rough rivers filled with enormous boulders. Everything was so hard and steep and severe and dangerous.

I've seen television shows featuring rock climbers looking for the ultimate extreme experience. They should come here.

We aren't used to the mountains or narrow, serpentine roads, and the drive actually was a bit scary. It seemed so easy to fall off a mountain or have a head-on collision, and unlike the main highway, the posted speed limits in the mountains seemed far too fast. We had to keep pulling over so other cars could pass.

Perhaps the fast drivers were used to the roads; perhaps they had cabins there and regularly made the drive. Norwegians, I am discovering, have a real love of the outdoors and often take advantage of it at their cabins, which they call "hytter." A weekend away at one is considered to offer the ultimate in sport, rest and relaxation. Some can only be gotten to on ski or snowshoe; many don't have heat or even running water. It is becoming clear to me that Norwegians are very close to nature and that in fact nature to them may be a kind of religion.

When we got to the hotel we were a bit giddy from the drive and we enjoyed having a drink as soon as we got in. Dinner was served, a buffet, with roast beef, vegetables and other hearty, standard fare. We still don't care much for the taste of meat here, but we eat it anyway. How else will we get used to it. The place, by the way, was set up nicely for children. They had a room with tables for coloring and a television with a VCR and lots of cartoons going. The kids were all happy to be together.

In the morning we realized we weren't going to be able to downhill ski with the kids. It was a bit of an oversight, but we hadn't been active in this way since having Ellen. We've been living in Houston since she was a baby and our sporty excursions as a family have been limited really to hiking and biking. So we scratched our alpine ski rentals and picked up cross-country. Ellen had her own skis and Peter went in the backpack, on George.

Ellen was able to ski! She had never tried and she did just fine. I was told Norwegians like to get children on skis as early as possible; at least by the time they are four. We saw plenty of young kids excelling at skiing, and other smaller ones being pulled on pods designed for the purpose. The pod-sleds, called "pulk," are these windproof capsules made cozy and warm with sheepskins and blankets and down sleeping bags. The children inside appear warm and content, though I was told there is some danger of freezing. This is all so unlike anything we've seen before.

In the end we didn't ski that much really but we enjoyed ourselves, meeting people, seeing new things and being outside in the weather. George and I used to cross country ski around Chicago and at school where we both studied, at the University of Wisconsin. Though we've come here from a warm climate and definitely prefer one, we know the one way to tolerate the cold is to be very active in it. There is some good kind of feeling you get overcoming the weather and actually being comfortable in it. I don't think the weather here is really that cold, but as it's always very wet, it really does seem to chill down deep.

We were the only Americans at the hotel, so we met lots of Norwegians. The children made a really nice effort with Ellen and some of them were speaking to her in English, including one ten-year-old boy who was very capable in English from what he'd learned just in school and from the Cartoon Network. And I thought there was nothing of value to be gotten from the Cartoon Network. I even had a chance to use my very limited Norwegian. I ordered a drink and billed it to my room number. You've got to start somewhere.

Friday night I went to bed early with the kids and George stayed up late socializing. Then Saturday night I got to go downstairs and have fun too, while he hit the sack early with the children, and at 3:45 in the morning we were all woken up by the ringing of a very loud bell. George and I sat up for a minute then realized it must be the fire alarm. I threw on my robe and boots and wrapped Peter in his comforter. George wrapped up Ellen and we headed for the stairs. We passed a lady in the stairwell and asked if she knew what was going on. She couldn't understand us.

We got down to the lobby and waited as everyone piled in. It was hard to know what was going on because the fire alarm was very loud and everyone was talking in Norwegian. The fire department arrived and looked around for awhile. They came down and announced that melting snow had caused a false alarm.

It sounds like nothing now but it was kind of scary to not know what was happening and the event has further solidified my decision to learn Norwegian.

Once everything was OK we all kind of looked around at each other with relief before going back up to bed. And here all around us in the lobby were the people we'd just sat up socializing with, but now they were in various states of undress. Men and women in just a t-shirt or sweater. No pants. A blanket on. And then there was me, looking very American, very puritanical, in very cute floral pajamas (with pants on, thank you) and a matching robe over it.

And just as an aside, earlier that evening I was telling some sympathetic listeners about my getting-lost episode going to Ellen's school. They told me there really isn't a good way to get to her school from where I was. They also told me that the reason I was confused about where I was—the road did say 510—was that I wasn't on 510. When the sign for the road has a box around the number, then you're on the road. The one I was on had a box with a kind of dotted line around the number. That meant I was on a road that leads to the road I wanted, but it wasn't the road. If I hadn't have stopped at the gas station I would have found what I needed eventually. So now at least I understand why I thought I was on 510 and why nothing looked familiar. Pretty important thing to know. Too bad I had to learn the hard way.

Speaking of driving, George actually thinks he has a right to be upset with me because I smashed the side window off the rental car. If you could only see the tiny garage door at the apartment you would agree it would take a Ph.D. in physics to get it right absolutely every time without hitting something. Wouldn't you know I would do it now, too, when the rental car is due back tomorrow and I finally get my own car.

And let me tell you about a funny thing that happened, before I close. I was driving along in the car, and suddenly I was overcome by the horrendous odor of, well, feces. For a few years now I've been used to smells that can happen in diapers. Never before had I smelled one, though, that was this bad. I actually pulled over. There on the side of the road I laid Peter down and began to change his diaper.

But I was so confused when I got into it and found nothing there. I felt like I might vomit from the horrendous smell, but if not the diaper, where was that smell coming from? Now I went right home and called Christin, and she told me the smell, which is still there, is actually pig and hen waste, and the farmers put it down as fertilizer. It is the heaviest, worst smell ever to offend my senses. It has even interfered with my ability to eat. Christin claims the smell will only be around for a few weeks.

I wonder what someone who is just visiting now thinks of this town.

Saturday, April 11

Tomorrow is Easter and Stavanger has been shut down since Wednesday afternoon. It won't open up again until next week. Løkkeveien Video, some restaurants and the Esso station by our apartment are about all that's open. No one is around and it is pretty depressing. One interesting thing, though, Christin had us for dinner and she served Easter moose!

I've never had to stock up on food before, being from the land of the 24-hour everything. But this Easter eating is about all we've done. And walking. I can't believe that now, just as things are seeming like spring, is the big time to ski. Apparently skiing doesn't really get going until the end of January, though the snow begins to fall in November. At least November 1 is when you put the tires with the metal studs on the car. The second Monday after Easter is when you take them off.

While most people are up in the mountains, others have taken trips to warmer climates, though no place very near here would really be that warm. We would have made plans to go somewhere except we didn't know Stavanger would turn into a ghost town for a week. Besides, where would we go? We just got here.

I read somewhere that no self-respecting Norwegian stays home at Easter and I will not forget that next year. For now we are among the very few seeing the sights. And in fact being in a ghost town has its benefits. I hit the bank just before it closed. Our contact there was just finishing things up in his office and he had his dog in there with him. Have you ever seen a dog in a bank? Anyway I was just finalizing things with the registration for the new car and I had the matter of a giro to tend to.

A giro, by the way (pronounced SHEE-roe if you are from these parts), is the Norwegian version of a check. If you get a bill it comes in the form of a giro. You write the amount in, if it isn't already printed on the giro, you put your bank account number on it, then sign it. It's different from the way we use checks in the United States, though. As far as I know they don't originate from you, and no one would ever personally give you one, such as how in the United States you might get a check for your birthday from your parents. You would not use a giro to pay for something while you are in a store. They can just show up in your mailbox, though, not even in an envelope or anything. But when I gave them my ownership forms, the folks at the Department of Motor Vehicles gave me the giro.

"What's this for?"

"Just take it to your bank then bring it back here."

"O.K." That's how everything works around here.

So I did get to the Department of Motor Vehicles hours before the Easter holiday began. Who goes then? Nobody. I was in and out in a jiff. And now I am finally done with the rental with the faulty side mirror and I have my own new bluish-green Volvo station wagon. We had the choice of bringing our cars from the United States with us, both Volvos, paying to have them shipped of course, and for modifications for use here. We solicited lots of advice from people. There are numerous factors, but the most important one is that you can't sell the car here before two years. We wondered what would happen if we want to leave before then. In short, we decided taking the cars could be too great a risk, and so in the end we sold them. But cars are incredibly expensive here, perhaps twice the price of the United States. We figure we probably should have kept and shipped at least one of our cars, but, shall I say it? Hindsight is 20/20.

So I'm tooling around in my new station wagon with nobody else on the road. We've been hitting the museums and we've seen nearly all of them. On Thursday we went to the fascinating Archeology Museum and saw lots of Viking artifacts and the 10,000 year-old bones of a polar bear found very near where we are living. Hey those are really old bones. There were lots of things for the kids to interact with and we ended up making a day of the museum for lack of anything else to do really. The thing is we met another really nice Norwegian family there, the Villards, spent the better part of the day with them, and we will try to see them again.

And yesterday we did the biggest tourist draw in the area. We took the ferry up the Lysefjord and saw something amazing which nature created called the Pulpit Rock. The rocks here are truly amazing, very vertical, and along the fjords they are probably at their most spectacular. You take the ferry along for an hour and a half or so, oohing and aahing until you are directly under a cliff that rises straight up 2,000 feet. On top of it is a flat table hanging out over the water. It looks like a priest's pulpit, hence the name, and it is a true feast for the eyes. All the while they play very dramatic music, and you can't help but choke up a bit it is so incredibly beautiful.

My sister, Debbie, is a classical oboist and she would be proud of me because I know what music was being played while we gasped over the Pulpit. It was Edvard Grieg's Peer Gynt Suite I, Op. 46, In the Hall of the Mountain King. If you know the piece you will immediately understand how the dramatic music so beautifully fit the dramatic scenery. Don't think I know a lot about music, by the way. I was on a Norwegian-themed activities kick before I moved here, to sort of help me gear up for things. Grieg, if you haven't surmised, was Norwegian. I also read some Henrik Ibsen plays, Scandinavian folk and fairy tales, and looked at some picture books featuring Norwegian artists, especially Edvard Munch.

And after all that, today is the day before Easter and we had endeavored to hoof it up a small mountain called Dalsnuten in neighboring Sandnes to enjoy the panoramic view of all the surrounding towns and the Ryfylke fjords. We were with our usual companions, Christin and her family.

What a crazy thing happened though. Perhaps just another spring day to everyone else, but we were incredulous as it began then just kept on snowing and snowing and snowing. Let me remind you today is April 11. Right now in Houston the only comfortable clothing is nearly naked. We're not as prepared as the locals here, who always have every conceivable change of clothing in their cars so they are always ready for anything.

Very unfortunately for us, too, was the fact that yesterday George, in a rare moment of non-procrastination, took the snow tires off the car. The roads were so slippery we got stuck, stuck, stuck and couldn't make it home. We got a push to Christin's house and waited it out at her place until things cleared up. We were there the whole day, wearing cozy, dry, borrowed clothes and keeping warm with coffee by the fire. I understand now why Norwegians like to ski at Easter. Lots of snow!

Tuesday, April 15

On top of the white Easter, Sunday was a disastrous day. George and I were fighting and the baby was cranky. Ellen was bored. The apartment got smaller and of course nothing was open and all we could do was sit around and look at each other. I thought to call someone to find out where I could go to a Catholic mass in English, but then I remembered everyone was away and I didn't feel I could possibly call Christin for one more thing. It was the first time in my life I missed going to church on Easter.

None of our friends or family in the United States called to wish us good tidings on our first holiday out of the country. If anyone sent a card we wouldn't have gotten it because there's been no mail delivered around here for days.

Yesterday, Monday, was the last official day of Easter (it is a fully sanctified six-day holiday here) and I went out by myself for a walk around Mosvatnet and a much-needed chance to sort out my head. I decided to stay out until I felt better and was ready to be in the company of my family again. I was out the whole morning.

When I got home I was calm but I looked at George and felt it best to leave again. I grabbed the kids and went out to see what might be open. All I could find was McDonald's and the children were delighted with that. So they chomped away on their Happy Meals oblivious to my very, very low mood. My mind was racing: I no longer like my husband, Norway stinks, everyone in the United States has forgotten us…

Then Jerome, who picked us up from the airport the day we arrived, came in to McDonald's. I think he could see right away that things weren't right. I confessed the situation. He listened thoughtfully.

I said, "I really don't think the problem is Norway. I think it's my husband. I just don't like him. He's driving me crazy."

Jerome looked at me and said something like this: You're going through a low point. It happens to everyone, I promise. This won't be the last time you feel like this. Things will probably get better once you move into your house. Stick it out. It's OK. You'll be all right.

That's exactly what I needed to hear and when we returned home everything was in fact already a bit better and we went out for a walk. Lots of walking I know but really there is little else to do. The art museum was actually open on Easter Sunday and so we stopped in. There was a terrific new exhibit on of the work of August Jacobsen, a Stavanger painter who lived from 1868 until 1955. Everything was so bright and optimistic and hopeful and it made me feel so happy.

As George hadn't in fact been in the museum before he was surprised to see the rest of it. It's all really so dark. There's a painting of a waiter named Gustav who's hanged himself. Another victim of an Easter in Stavanger, perhaps?

Later April 15

I got a call from my dear, darling, wonderful best friend Kirste. It was so good to hear her voice and tell her how awful things have been. George and I were so angry with everyone for not calling us we came up with the idea of a contest to reward the first person that cared about us enough to call. We would buy that person a Norwegian sweater. So I told Kirste I won't rest until I've found the most beautiful sweater in Norway and sent it to her.

Wednesday, April 22

Can you believe it's finally moving day? George is at our new house at Sandal Terrasse 33 with the movers. Ellen is at school and I have just finished loading up the station wagon with all the mess from the apartment, and the baby.

Things are fine. While Easter was a real low point things do seem to be improving now. The plain truth is doing anything here is really such a chore and quite an effort. Is that what they mean by culture shock? Of course I've read all about that. They say culture shock is the stress that results from an inability to organize your life because of the unfamiliarity and uncertainty in your surroundings. Ellen always says, "Everything is different in Norway." It is. I just thought if I knew enough about culture shock it couldn't blindside me.

The thing is, everything I do here I do like an idiot. I am sure in fact that everyone I come across in a day thinks I am an idiot. It's hard to be cool when you don't know what's going on. It really would help if I knew the language, but that won't happen overnight. I've barely mastered my numbers at this point.

But just take as an example of the difficulties here my recent experiences at the gas station. First I go into the station because my credit card won't work at the pump. I have had problems since I moved here paying for anything because none of my American cards seem to work anywhere and my new local bank still has not mailed my debit card. So I go into the station and the woman inside seems to speak English well enough. I show her my card and tell her it won't work in the machine. No problem, she says. I ask her if I have to pay before I pump. Very confused look. No.

Then I realize that's a good thing because I have absolutely no idea how much gas my new car will take or what it might cost. I still haven't gotten kroner straight in my head (7.5 is really not an easy number to divide by), and I don't have a clue how many gallons my new tank will hold, let alone liters. The price of gas of course is based on liters—is it two liters, or four, to the gallon—and it's times like this I wish I had paid more attention when we worked on the metric system in Junior High.

So I feel relieved I don't have to figure all this out first and I just go out and fill the tank. I finish up and when I do the math in my head I'm pretty sure this fill up has just cost me nearly $70. I go back in and my credit card doesn't work in her machine either, and she has to get an old hand-operated credit card machine and she can't find the slips that go with it.

The next time I stop in I'm loaded down with cash and I'm due for a wash too. There's no hose at the apartment and the car's a mess from all the snow. When I go in to pay the same woman is working behind the register. I tell her I need a wash but this time she no longer seems to speak English. Mustering up my best after six weeks of Norwegian language lessons, I offer: "bil vask." She nods in understanding, then asks which kind I want. Of course I have absolutely no idea. I know there's no use asking what the options are, because I won't understand them anyway and then she says in English,

"You want the best."

"OK, what does that cost?" And it turns out it costs over $11. What?

In the end I take the best because I don't know what else to do. I consider taking out a loan to pay for the gas and the wash, but pay with cash in the end. She hands me a card that I examine with some curiosity and I walk out. Apparently it is for the wash. So I pull my car up to the door of the car wash machine, but there is a car already parked in front of me. It isn't running with anyone in it or anything, it is actually parked. I sit behind it for awhile then give up, assuring myself that this kind of crap never happens in the United States.

I drive to Ellen's school because I'm worried I might be late. Lord knows how long I might have sat waiting behind a parked car, and I don't want to be late to school again either. So I pick her up, socialize a bit with the other moms, and when I get back it's about 40 minutes later. The parked car is gone and I drive right up. I try to put the card into the machine and it keeps coming back out. There is some message but I can't read it. I decide it must be that I was gone so long the card has expired. So I go back into the station. The lady is still there. I tell her the card doesn't work and about the parked car and how I had to go to school to pick up Ellen. She looks at me for a long time. I am pretty sure she thinks I've been out there 40 minutes trying to get the car wash to work.

So she gets some guy to come out from the back to help me. He puts the card into the machine and the door opens instantly. He gives me a look I don't care for and I drive in. The automated wash begins and I see in my rear view window that a taxi has pulled into the line behind me. The driver is out of the car talking to the guy who helped me. I am imagining their conversation about how I tried for 40 minutes before asking for help and I wonder what on earth ever made me think it would be fun to live in a foreign country.

The wash goes on and on. Thanks goodness I picked up Ellen first! In the United States a car wash costs a couple of bucks and lasts a couple of minutes. I start to think of a commercial I've seen recently where a couple is having sex in the car while it's in an automated wash like this one. In fact I think it just might be possible, the wash is taking so long. But finally it ends and I start up the car. Silly me, I never turned it off! The sound of my engine being over-started in the tiny confines of the car wash was so very, very loud. I didn't even bother to look back at the taxi driver or the gas station attendant to see if they noticed.

Just remember this: Every time I do anything, the simplest thing, it's this difficult.

Thursday, April 23

George's birthday today. Happy birthday, I love you. Boxes, boxes, boxes are everywhere. But we managed to avoid them. We put on a few sweaters and ate a very nice dinner on the terrace. It was cool but sunny and the view is so fine.

One new thing to report going on in the neighborhood. I took the children to the park by my house yesterday and a number of people were working on the landscaping there. Two people were speaking French, and this confused me. Why would French people move to Norway to do labor jobs? Both are socialist countries with very high standards of living. So I asked. Due to the nature of the socialist system here, it turns out any kind of labor is super expensive. In the neighborhoods, at the schools and everywhere, people gather together and do the work themselves. It's called a "dugnad." Incidentally, it's a great way to meet the neighbors. The French people, by the way, are expats too.

And on a very trivial note: I just found out Snoopy is known as Sniff here.

Monday, May 4

Life continues to be a challenge but I sure do like my house. We moved in a week and a half ago. All went well. Nothing important was broken or lost. The movers picked up most of the empty boxes, not that we're at all settled mind you, but I can see this is going to be the place for us.

What is really fantastic is the location. The lake we're on, Stokkavatnet, is really, really lovely. We have a fabulous view of it and the hills around it and it's steps from our door. It's all so natural and beautiful and I'm feeling very, very happy.

The weather has been in the 60s and we've started to see the sun. We have a terrace that wraps nearly all the way around the house and when it is sunny I can usually find some place to sit where I can enjoy the sun protected from the wind. The thing is the wind really does whip, and sometimes it sounds like there's a train running past the house, it's howling so loud and the windows actually are rattling and shaking.

And since I'm complaining, we made the mistake of walking the five miles around Stokkavatnet for the first time on a very windy day. Then it started to rain. Then it really rained. Unfortunately we had the kids with us. Peter was in his stroller and Ellen was in the Baby Jogger—that's one of those big three-wheeled jobbies you can run behind, for the unknowing. Everyone's wheels kind of got really stuck in the mud. It was very hard to push. We had to collapse our umbrellas because we needed to commit two hands each to pushing the strollers. We weren't used to the hills either. Then we turned a curve, wind was full in our faces and we were really fighting it. What a nightmare!

Our five-mile walk took us over two and-a-half hours, pretty pathetic. And I thought we were in good shape. George has run two marathons for heaven's sake. But now we have resolve. With this lovely lake just outside our door we must get very, very fit, just like all the Norwegians we see around us, biking to work in a heavy rain, using some sort of ski-Roller Blade thingies with cross-country ski poles, alongside the highway. Do they ever drive anywhere? Already George has tackled the lake three more times since our first venture, running around it, each time going faster and faster. Then our neighbor Olaf told us he has run around it in 37 minutes. Good grief!

But I digress. Life is generally good for us here. Let me take a minute to tell you how Ellen is doing. When she started back at her new preschool after Easter I watched her run into the classroom, leap into her teacher's lap and kiss her full on the lips. I loved seeing that. Then I watched the other children doing much the same. Certainly they love their teacher. Is this sort of demonstrative behavior practiced or encouraged in the United States? Well I don't know for sure but I think there are probably rules, if not laws, prohibiting it.

To that end I also think the Norwegians must be much less litigious than Americans. Well, probably the whole rest of the world is. The thing is you can see it in what people can do. Everything is more dangerous, there is more chance to be injured, and nobody worries about it. I see kids balancing along a high fence at the daycare next to Ellen's school. The fence must be six feet tall and the kids are six or five years old, walking along there with adults present, but not assisting. Not even interested. In the neighborhood kids are always playing up on the roofs, walking along the edge, throwing things off.

Ellen has been sewing finger puppets at school, which seems a bit dangerous for a four-year-old, with a real needle and thread, and I asked, "What do you do if you prick your finger?"

"I put it in my mouth."

"Does it ever bleed?"

"Well yeah."

She regularly bakes or cooks at school too. Every Tuesday.

"Have you ever burned yourself?"

"Not really very much."

Maybe the kids learn more faster with all their freedom. There are lots and lots of tree forts in our neighborhood, and some of them aren't in people's yards but on public property. This is apparently no problem. People swim and skate on the lake. I read that Norway has the highest rate of childhood accidents in the world.

At home Ellen is also allowed to do as she pleases. She plays in the street, she is allowed to walk to the park and play there by herself. She can ride her bike wherever she likes, which sounds more permissive than it is because there are very big hills around here and that in itself limits biking. But she is having a blast, and we did spy her up on a roof with some other kids and I said, I think it's OK, but her father went over and yelled at her. A short time later I saw her back up there.

The neighborhood children, of whom there are many, have been very interested in us. They're not sure what to think; though they don't seem to mind Ellen. We've got a playroom that could rival F.A.O. Schwartz, and some of them have seen it, but they are a bit standoffish and the doorbell rarely rings. The young ones don't understand our attempts to speak Norwegian at all, and they are very confused when we don't understand them either.

We did the American thing and went around and introduced ourselves to our neighbors as soon as we moved in. I don't think you really do that here, but we did. Nobody screamed or ran away, and people are being friendly back. Whenever I go out I have a little chat with somebody and I'm coming to know some of the adults, especially across the street, next door. They keep saying things like, "You're so nice, you know we never talked to anyone from that house before …"

But all that said, and despite the fact I feel I'm making a really major effort every day in everything I do, I get down very easily. I have considered it and I'm sure I'm one of the most outgoing people I know. Just when I think things are getting better, though, something happens to really bring me down. Then I start to think of my friends and the good life I had in the United States and how easy it all was.

We've been in Norway over two months now, and I wonder how much longer all this effort will have to go on. Well, it can't be forever. My dad has lived in the United States for decades, having moved there from Austria when he was a younger man, and I never hear him talking about culture shock. Although now that I really think about it, how many times have I heard him say, "Well, you know back in the Old Country …"

Evening, Friday, May 15

Today was Peter's first birthday. Happy Birthday to my dear little angel. I am happy over the occasion but also sad—he turned one kind of all alone. For Ellen's first birthday my parents had a big party with balloons, a fancy cake and 30 people came to celebrate with her. Today it was just the four of us and some uncertainty that George would even make it. He'd been in Scotland.

I've continued with unpacking and things have been quiet but nice and recently we had our new friends the Villards—the ones we met at the Archeology Museum—over for, well, I'm not sure what it was but the company was very good. What started as a walk with the kids around the lake ended as a lunch though we really weren't prepared for it, food-wise or from a tidiness point of view, what with the boxes and everything. The thing is, the couple, Ingvill and Tore, are as easy going and casual as we are. They have a boy roughly Ellen's age, a girl Peter's age, and one in the middle, a girl who I think is about three and a half. They might make very nice friends for us.

Tore and Ingvill are originally from Oslo, they have lived in the United States, and I can tell they like America and Americans. Perhaps that's why we like them. Tore works for a helicopter company, and I only just learned helicopters can carry up to 18 people. I had no idea, but now I know that is how people who work offshore on the oil platforms get out there. I guess it's a bit dangerous too. All the passengers on the helicopter have to wear survival suits during the flights.

And although she is Norwegian, Ingvill reminds me very much of my friends in the United States. Like me, she has spent her professional life in public relations. She currently works out of her home doing translation and publicity for a French cosmetics company. She gave me good advice about things kid-related and has really encouraged me with my Norwegian language efforts (I really appreciate it when people do that), and I had her write down some Norwegian words I was having trouble with into a book I carry around. I also had her write her children's names in it. As I understand the Norwegian alphabet better it is very helpful for me to see things written down. The children's names, by the way, are Didrik, Martine and Pernille.

I have the names of lots of people written in that book, and I frequently ask my Norwegian teacher, Astrid, for help on the names. I'm always grateful, too, that Norwegians have these little plaques by their front doors with the names of all the family members listed. Then while I wait for them to answer the door I have a moment to refresh my memory and practice my pronunciation.

My work with Norwegian is going pretty well I think, and I am really enjoying the time I spend in the classroom and working at home. I think my teacher is very good, I see her every week and she is becoming a friend too. Through her I've learned so much about Norwegian culture, not just the language, and she's also the one who keeps me up to date on what's happening around here locally.

Astrid has taught at elementary school for 30 years. She started teaching what we call kindergarten, then stayed with that class for four years. She's done this cycle over and over for years now. When she told me that, I was so surprised because we don't do anything like that in the United States, and while I can see some merit to the system, staying with all the same people the first few years, I also can come up with some drawbacks and I still haven't come to any conclusion on the whole idea. What is interesting to me is that just a couple of years ago they made a change in regards to when children begin school. It used to be age seven, but now your child can begin at age six if you prefer.

And let me tell you a few things I've learned about the language. To start, in Norwegian they have three more letters than we do: æ, ø and å. They come at the very end of the alphabet and they, plus a, e, i, o, u and y, are the vowels. The "æ" is pronounced kind of like the noise Ellen makes when she's sneaking up on me. Sort of like "eahhh." Actually, I think it's pronounced very much like the "a" in our word "at."

The "ø," it's pronounced kind of "euh." Maybe it sounds a bit like the "i" in our word "bird." It's in a word I think is so hilarious, "kjøkken," which means kitchen, and is pronounced roughly "sheuh ken," with a bit of a pause between the syllables. Other words that start with kind of a "sh" sound begin with ki, tj, sj, skj and sometimes sk. The sound of the "sh" changes a bit, depending on where your tongue is and the shape you form with your mouth.

The last letter, "å," sounds like "aw." The name Paul is here spelled Pål, but pronounced exactly the same way we do it. I have also come across someone with the last name Vån, and it's pronounced exactly like my last name, Vaughan. And speaking of personal names, that's about the only time they use a capital letter here. They also don't use an apostrophe for possessives. And they don't use titles when they speak to people, like Mr., Mrs., Professor or whatever. I understand you can get an idea of where someone is from by the way they pronounce their "r." In Oslo it's a roller and around here it's more guttural like the French "r." And speaking of Oslo, around here it is pronounced sort of "Ah sloo." If you're from there you say "Ash loo."

The language in general has a real singsong quality to it, with lots of ups and downs in intonation and pauses even mid-word for emphasis. Do you remember the Swedish Chef from the Muppet Show, where he wasn't actually speaking Swedish, just what people think Swedish sounds like? Well Norwegian kind of sounds like the Swedish Chef too.

And let me just tell you a thing or two about Norwegian nouns. Well for one thing I have a lot of them to learn. Like German and French, two languages I have also studied, Norwegian nouns take their own special article, either masculine, feminine, neutral or plural. As I recall from studying German and French, it takes a long time to learn which words take which article. I never worried about it too much speaking those languages, and I'm sure I made lots of mistakes. But you'll never learn anything if you don't try. My motto is, there's no place for pride when speaking a foreign language!

The article in Norwegian, by the way, is used a bit differently in that it can be attached to the end of a word. Let me give you an example. They use the word "film" just as we do, meaning "movie." "A film" is "en film." "The film" is "filmen," and "the films" is "filmene." For plural nouns the regular rule is to just add "er," whereas we would use "s." So the English plural of film, "films," would be "filmer" in Norwegian.

And besides the "kj" like you find in the word "kjøkken," and all the other "sh" sounding words, they also have another unlikely letter combination, which is "gj." It's pronounced "yuh," kind of like our "y." There is a sign in the parking lot at my old apartment which reads "gjeste-parkering," pronounced "YES te par KER ring," and it means "guest parking." It certainly makes life easier that I am becoming able to read the signs around me.

It also helps to be able to understand a bit of Norwegian so you can get an idea of what to expect with the weather. Well, I think all you really need to know is the word "dårlig," which means "bad." When you watch the television news or look at a newspaper, though, you'll sometimes come across the word "oppholdsvær," which fascinates me, as there is actually the need for such a word. It means "not raining." So you may see that you can expect a day of not raining. But that would be unlikely.

So these are just a few things I know about the Norwegian language now, and I know I have a very long way to go before I can really speak and read Norwegian. I'm convinced we'll all be better off here, not to mention happier, when we can communicate with people and read the things around us. When learning to speak a foreign language, the best thing to do is just use it as much as you can. You'll make lots of mistakes, but who cares? When I was a student in France people thought my mistakes were cute. Every now and then I would say something and a smile would unexpectedly go around the room. Who cares? Life is long if you're lucky. Some of those years you can be cool, sometimes you have to just let things be, and let everyone think you are a total idiot. It's really no big deal.

The problem is that here in Norway, except for the very old and the very young, virtually everyone speaks a bit of English, and many speak it flawlessly. I can see the temptation to not even bother, and it's also easy to slip into English the first moment you can't immediately think of how to say something. Ellen, on the other hand, as a four-year old, does not have this luxury. Four-year-old Norwegian kids do not speak English. Her life will be better when she can speak to our neighbors. She needs to have a good life here. And I feel if I expect her to learn to speak Norwegian, I must set a good example and do it myself. How else could we have the neighborhood children over to our house, either? It's so cute when I do my homework. She pretends to do hers too.

I am learning there are some expat assignments where people don't learn the language or try at all to fit in, not for lack of interest but because it's just too different. I hear the Middle East is often like that. People I know have really enjoyed assignments there. The climate is hot but sunny. Everyone lives near each other in a special area or compound. There's lots of time for improving the tennis game and shopping. But the only society anyone really is part of is the small expat community.

We've also met expats here working with NATO. They are used to living on a base, moving every few years, and mostly socializing with other NATO people. I guess with moving as often as they do, it's simplest for them to keep to themselves. I don't think they could manage learning a new language every couple of years. But not integrating makes it harder for them to be here, too, I think.

And all this brings to mind a very real and serious problem that's going on right now in Indonesia. We've followed in the news stories about student protests and an economic and social collapse that is taking place there. We've just learned that some friends of ours who live there, an American family with four children, have been sent out of the country for reason of safety. I begin to wonder if it's really such a good idea to do any of this expat stuff at all.

Saturday, May 16

The weather was sunny, about 65 F, and I walked around Stokka in an hour and a half. That's real improvement there.

I feel I'm becoming more fit, and it's not hard to be outside getting fit because spring has sprung and it's so beautiful outside! Every day we see bright new leaves and wildflowers are coming up and things are just growing and lush and lively and lovely. Babies ducklings are swimming behind their mothers on the lake and everywhere there is new life and things are great.

Evening, Sunday, May 17

Today is May 17, Norway's Constitution Day. It's sort of like our Independence Day, only just a bit confusing. Perhaps I can clear things up with a very brief history lesson, as I understand the history anyway.

Norway was made up of many little kingdoms until about 1075 A.D., when a battle was fought between three of the Viking kings, and Harald Hårfagre was the victor. He became the first true king of Norway and I think I mentioned all this a while back when I told you about the Three Swords monument at Hafrsfjord. As far as I can make out, the Black Death, which arrived in the middle of the fourteenth century, wiped out much of the Norwegian population (not to mention the population of Europe) and many of the prosperous estates and great farms could no longer be properly maintained. Pretty much everybody had to scratch out a living, because all the labor force was dead, and this, people speculate, may have given rise to the classless society that exists in Norway today.

Norway managed well enough through all this and remained independent until 1397, when on Trinity Sunday, the country was united with Sweden and Denmark. Perhaps it was the decimation of the noble class which made the partnership between Norway, Sweden and Denmark so likely. In any event, the three countries joined at the close of the fourteenth century, and they were together for 400 years. If you'll permit me to spare you the details of those years, I'll cut directly to Napoleon Bonaparte. I'm a bit sketchy on what actually happened but he was able to get Norway and Denmark to join him in attacking Sweden, in the early 19th century.

Then in 1814, following his defeat at Leipzig, the Peace of Kiel was written and signed. Through it Denmark paid off its war debt by giving up Norway. And Sweden and Norway were joined. What confuses me is why Norway, while in union with Sweden, would come up with its own constitution (on May 17, 1814), but they did. And on the same day they also elected a king, but they did not part from Sweden until 1905, nearly a century later. So while Norway wasn't actually independent until just 93 years ago, what they celebrate on May 17th is the constitution they came up with and signed back in 1814.

Did you follow that?

Well Constitution Day today is a children's day. For a couple of weeks I've watched school children out around our house practicing for the parade, and Ellen has been out with her school practicing in Sola, the town where her school is located. Those are the festivities we participated in.

We walked along the streets of Sola behind the Children's House parade float, which was decorated with lovely little spring twigs and flags from around the world. We enjoyed the parade in the opposite way one normally would; we walked in the parade, and observed with interest the people standing on the sides of the street watching.

And quite the opposite of the American Fourth of July, where everyone wears a bit of red, white and blue and t-shirts and shorts, even cut-offs are acceptable, the thing to have on today is a "bunad," the formal, traditional folk costume of Norway. As nothing is simple in Norway, neither is the bunad. There are an infinite variety of styles, colors and accessories, but there are some commonalities too.

For women, the bunad comprises a long, full wool skirt covered in lovely embroidery, an elaborate, lacy linen blouse, a vest, possibly a cape, and some kind of hat. All this is made all the fancier with the addition of many little dangling silver accessories: pins, buttons and chains, which decorate the vest and blouse and often are passed down through the generations or given as gifts for very special occasions. I believe a woman's costume costs about $5,000 to buy in a store, not including the accessories, and some people do make them at home. A young woman might get one to wear first for her Confirmation, and she could also wear it as her wedding dress and at any occasion throughout her lifetime where formal attire is in order.

The whole thing is very convertible, too, to accommodate pregnancies and the occasional ups and downs, ins and outs, women experience with their figures over the years. The linen blouse is the only thing that might need to be replaced. I saw one in a shop in town and it was $500. It all sounds a bit extravagant but really it's practical because if you take good care of your bunad, not only can you wear it your whole life, your granddaughter can wear it too.

The men's bunad is a lovely thing also, which compliments the woman's. It features a similar white linen shirt; lots of silver buttons and either regular-length wool pants or a shorter version which stops just below the knee. With it a man can wear either a vest or jacket, or both, special knit socks and shoes with silver buckles. The total look is about as stunning as seeing a man all decked out in a formal Scottish kilt. Very handsome, very sexy.

I had heard during a presentation about traditional Norwegian folk costumes (at a Conoco wives club meeting I attended) that each town has its own bunad. I got a free poster from the local newspaper, the Stavanger Aftenblad, which I still can't begin to read incidentally, and it presents 19 different costumes for our county alone. And you don't even necessarily wear the bunad from your county. You may prefer to wear the bunad of Telemark, for example, where your mother is from. So there's a lot of variety.

And, lest you forgot, we saw all these bunads on the people who were watching us walk in the parade. I know it sounds crazy. A couple of months ago we had never even been to Norway and already this, in a parade, and I was surprised I actually was able to wave at some people I knew along the way. When we got to the end the kids all ate the ever-present and super-delicious Norwegian ice cream and we listened to some music. Then we headed to Christin's.

Christin's family was all there and so we got to meet a lot of her relatives. We also ate from a nice buffet and drank some wine. In all it was a lovely day, the weather was sunny and warm, just perfect really, and flags were waving everywhere, the fjord was sparkling, and people were all so happy and I can see why it is a day so special to Norwegian people.

Friday, May 22

The wind has been blowing from the north for a few days and its been cold, gray and unpleasant. It seems like the weather has such an effect on things. Certainly it seems to have one on me, and I was feeling kind of bad for no reason, and then I got one. George came home and told me that things weren't working out with one of his co-workers in Houston who had taken one of our two cats when we moved here.

We had the cats for years and we very attached to them. But we found out that to bring them to Norway would mean a six-month quarantine in Oslo for both of them. The ridiculously high cost to bring them here (the flight, the quarantine), wasn't even an issue because we didn't think at their advanced ages, 13 and 15, they could handle half a year caged in isolation. So, in addition to selling our house and our cars we searched for homes for our cats.

For one of our cats finding a good home was very easy. Our dear friends the Woolers were over often and their daughter Rachel loved Goose, our big fluffy white one. We were sad to lose him but very happy that Rachel would get to have him, and we knew we would always be in touch. Our other cat, Boris—a slightly unattractive, fat, brown, striped, Siamese tomcat—well he was more of a problem.

I got him from an animal shelter where I used to volunteer in the 1980s. Boris is one of those cats that sat in a cage so long he ended up on special, the Featured Cat. I absolutely adored him at first sight, and have always loved him dearly. It broke my heart to part with him but I felt better knowing he was going to live with a friend of George's who is a real cat lover. But Boris didn't get along with her other cats and he started spraying and doing damage to her home. Needless to say, he had to go.

So we had to find a new home for him, from way over here in Norway. I've been working on this for several days. My dear, sweet, wonderful friend Margaret picked up Boris for me. She was going to hold on to him until we could figure out what to do. She has two dogs herself, so she couldn't keep him.

Margaret made so many phone calls for me and in the end drove Boris all the way to Natchez, Mississippi, where she is from, to give him to a family friend who has a farm. Now I'm torn between my sad feelings for abandoning my cat and moving here, and the very good ones I have realizing what a lucky person I am to have a friend who is so good to me.

I do have a lot of good friends, good old friends, but they are all so far away. So I'm sad for all sorts of reasons just now.

Monday, May 25

I've said before that everything is different in Norway and that even simple things are difficult. You can include the garbage in that.

We started having problems with our garbage the moment we arrived in Norway. In fact the person who is in charge of working with us on our housing called to say people at the apartment had complained that we were throwing out our garbage improperly.

Here's what we've been able to figure out up until now: Paper goes in the green bins which are picked up once a month. Most glass and plastic bottles go back to the store for a refund. You load up other plastic, metal and glass and you take it to a recycling receptacle where you sort it out and throw it in yourself. The rest goes in the black plastic garbage can that gets picked up on Friday, if you remember to put it out on the curb. Anything unusual, say something big that wouldn't fit into the black can, you take directly to the city dump yourself. I have no idea where that is.

The thing is in Houston I just chucked stuff into the garbage can and the guys who pick it up walked all the way up my driveway and picked it up. Twice a week. All recyclables, glass, metal, plastic and paper, went all together into the green bin. Once a week I hauled that thing down the driveway and forgot about it. No sorting, no putting stuff in my car.

Now when I drive around I always hear bottles clinking around because I have to drive them to the recycling station or back to the store, and while they often make it to the car, they seem to like to stay in there. I'm not perfect, and as a result I find I've got things piling up all over the place really. A day or two after we moved in here they had a paper recycling pick up, which I didn't know about and so I missed it. And because we had just moved in we had a lot of junk too, especially the paper my things were wrapped with. I also missed the first regular garbage pick up, because I didn't know about it, and actually when we moved in the cans were already full with the junk the old people threw out when they were moving.

So we've been absolutely swimming in garbage over here at Sandal Terrasse 33 pretty much since we moved in. And last week some plastic bags were left behind by the garbage men. Now at least we know that means there's a holiday coming up so they won't be by to pick up our garbage for awhile.

You must be wondering my point in all this and here it is: When you're new to a foreign country, it's not a good idea to wing it on your own and figure things out yourself. Sometimes you have to ask for help and sometimes you have to just let people help you. I am so very grateful to have had friends like Christin, Polly and Carolyn. They have helped me so much, but sometimes I feel guilty. Since I've gotten here I feel like all I do is take, take, take from people. It's not my nature. But I can't read my mail, so I have to ask for help. I can't figure out where horseradish is in the grocery store (in a toothpaste tube, in with specialty produce). Where's the Catholic Church? Do you know if they have masses in English? Can you help me with my cat? Help me, help me, help me.

That's why I didn't ask about the garbage. And what a mess that's been.

I continue to feel a bit frustrated and I guess it's even beginning to show. My daughter came to me recently with some questions. Here's how it went:

"Mama ."

"Yes dear."

"What does @*!?&@! mean?"

"Ellen! Don't ask me about that word. That's a bad, bad word and you shouldn't ever say it or think about it again. Please."

"But you say it."

"Oh. ... I'm very sorry about that, dear. Mommy is very wrong to say that. I have had a little more than I can handle lately. I will try very very hard not to say that any more. Please forgive me and please don't ever say that word. Please dear."

"Can I say !&#%!£?"

"No."

"Can I say %$?#?"

Oh %$?#!

Tuesday, May 26

What the @/&ø%@?!?!?!?!

Friday, May 29

Things, as perhaps you've noticed, have not been going very well. Everything is just really really bugging me!

Let me tell you what bugs me. The thing is they just don't share American views about what customer service is here. If you're lucky, the place where you are going will let you take a number. OK, it's fair at least. Sometimes I feel like I'm living in Russia or something with how long I have to wait in line, though. I just don't get it. Why not employ more people during your peak business times?

In fairness, when it finally is your turn the service is good.

But if you don't get to take a number, the crowds can be scary. People aren't necessarily as courteous as I'm used to, either. Here, if you are waiting in line at the bakery, and you were there first, it doesn't really matter. People who are most aggressive are served first. And Ellen and I were waiting in line to buy candy at the movie theatre one day and there was so much pushing and shoving.

She said, "Mommy, people keep bumping into me and it hurts."

What could I say.

I know it's a gross generalization, but people don't tend to be as courteous exiting theaters or other public places, where people normally file out. And if you need to use a toilet, even if you're first waiting in line, expect that someone will cut in front of you.

Picture this conversation, which may have taken place at a public ladies room anywhere. Understand that while I try to use my Norwegian all the time, it is not quite that of a native yet.

"Excuse me. I was here first."

"What?"

"I was here first."

"What?"

"I was here first."

"What are you saying?"

"Excuse me, but I was here first and I'm next."

"What?"

In English, "Give me a break."

Must be problems with the accent. Anyway, it's just a bit too aggressive around here. And people not acknowledging me, I find that awful. I'm used to strangers exchanging pleasantries with me when I'm out in public. I like my existence acknowledged in some way. People seem to go out of their way to hold a door open for you in the United States, and then they look at you and smile as you walk through. That's what I'm used to and that's how I like it.

OK, I admit I'm not feeling good about being here as much as I did when we first arrived, and I may be exaggerating a bit right now. But are these the kinds of cultural differences those books on expat living were talking about? Is this the stuff that can rock your world?

Another example, I'm at the Cultural Center and I'm waiting an eternity for someone to show up at the counter where they give you information about shows and events in town. I wait and wait and wait and wait for someone to show up. There is a woman who has been there since before me waiting too. As my kids are starting to grumble, I say to her, in Norwegian,

"Do you know if I can buy tickets here?" I was there to buy tickets for a play but why wait forever if I can't buy tickets there anyway, right. She seems very put off by the fact that I've spoken to her and says,

"I don't work here."

I tell her I realize that. Does she know, though? Well, I'll never find out because now she is ignoring me.

Then there's the fact that I have to run to 100 different shops to do my shopping. If I want a really nice cut of meat I go to the butcher. If I want cheddar cheese that is orange I have to go to a special cheese shop. If I want good produce I go to the green grocers. If I want wine I go to the Vinmonopolet. Of course I am used to being able to do all this at one place, right, and I'm not used to all the long lines, so of course I'm a bit irritated. How does any woman who works here manage to do all this stuff? At least I've got time, but what a way to waste it.

The worst thing recently involved saline solution for contact lenses. You can only buy it in two places, the drug store and an optical shop. I went into the drug store, where incidentally you have to take a number and wait in line whether you are getting a prescription or just buying something, and the line was waaaaay toooo loooong. So I went down to the eyeglass shop in the same complex. No one else was there, I picked up two bottles of saline solution ($10 each incidentally) and took them to the counter to pay for them. The saline solution was in fact located just next to the cash register. As I was turning my body with the bottles of saline solution in each hand, a woman ran in from the side and we met at the counter at precisely the same moment. I put the two bottles down on the counter and the woman behind the counter decided to help the other lady first, who was there to PICK OUT GLASSES!!!!

After the baby became fussy I said, "Can't I just pay for these?" The lady working there would not even look at me!

I was so mad and the thing is I really needed the saline solution, but I stormed out. But I'm not used to getting mad when I'm out shopping, I hate losing control, and now I don't even feel like going out at all. I'm really frustrated with things here. All the times I've smiled and pretended not to care, well it has all added together now and I just feel so irritated from the effort of doing the very simplest things.

Let me just tell one more story. I went into the dry cleaners to pick up some things. I rarely go to the cleaners in Norway because it costs a fortune. I mean it. It's $7.50 for a shirt, and it takes two weeks, can you believe it? The thing is I did have a few suits I just had to clean and I didn't have a choice about it. So I went back to pick the things up a few weeks later. (None of that same-day service here.) I walked in the door and said,

"Hi, my name is Vaughan. I've got some suits to pick up."

"Do you have a slip?"

"The one you gave me when I dropped off?" Good grief. It was over two weeks ago. Certainly I've added a number of slips, receipts, paper bits to my purse since then. So I start to look through my wallet, my coat pockets, then inside my purse. Eventually I've got the entire contents of my purse disassembled on the counter. And I've got really little kids so there's all kinds of junk in my bag, and I look up and say,

"Hey, come on. My name's Vaughan. I can't find my slip. Can't you just get my stuff?"

"I don't care what your name is. If you don't have a slip then I don't have your number. If I don't have your number I can't find your things."

"Are you kidding me?"

"No, but you're welcome to come back here and look through our inventory and find your stuff yourself."

"Are you kidding me?"

In the end I decided it best to just get out of there. As I stormed out my parting words were,

"You know, you and the video store should really get it together and put things in alphabetical order. Haven't you ever heard of customer service?"

She laughed.

When I got home I told George what happened and he said, "Didn't our dry cleaners in Chicago give us a bottle of champagne for Christmas one year?" Exactly!

Now listen, I know I sound like a real $&#!*%. I am not like this normally. My personal motto is to always be kind, respectful and supportive of all people always. If you can't say anything nice, don't say anything. But just trying to cope here, to do anything, and I've turned into an angry, raging lunatic. I know when I first got here I wasn't irritated by all this. Now I think I'm beginning to embarrass my daughter when we're in public. I'm having so much trouble now. What's going on?

And given my state regarding things just now, I probably made a big mistake choosing this week to go to the Legevakt. Do you remember I told you about the Legevakt? That's the doctor you go to if you are actually sick. It's for acute illness and it's a lot like going to the emergency room.

Anyway, Peter wasn't really sick. I knew what he had. He played with his friend Chloe and her mother called later saying a little rash was all over Chloe's hands, feet and mouth. She'd taken Chloe in and the Legevakt said it was hand, foot and mouth disease. Nothing at all serious, but very contagious.

So Peter came out with the same rash. I called to the Legevakt to get advice on what to do with it and they said, "You really should come in."

I didn't really think it sounded necessary but then I thought, hey, it's probably a good time to see what the Legevakt is all about. Then if I have a child in convulsions or dying or with a chopped off head or something sometime I will at least know what to do, what to expect. So we went.

We walked in the door and took a number. Nothing unusual there. We waited one hour and told a nurse what the problem was. She wrote some things down and then told us to take a second number. We then waited two more hours. The total wait to see a doctor was three hours. All the while Peter was exposed to some very sick people who were coughing, sneezing and crying all around us. I figured, if he isn't sick now, he will be in a few days. When it was our turn there were at least no surprises with the diagnosis.

The doctor looked him over and pronounced it foot, hand and mouth disease. He said he wouldn't recommend any special treatment.

Saturday, June 13

I got that hand, foot and mouth disease. It was awful. I ran a high fever and was sick in bed for a week. Then I got a really bad sinus infection. I went to the doctor. He said,

"Yes, I can see your ear is really infected."

He told me to do nothing but rest. He didn't give me any antibiotics or any other medicine. This is the sort of thing that drives my American friends crazy.

I chock my sad state of health to a depressed immune system, which is suffering under the weight of what I only now realize is a very huge deal, this moving-to-a-foreign-country thing. I guess we're about three-and-a-half months into it now, prime culture shock crisis time APPARENTLY. And on top of feeling poorly, I can barely stand my husband.

I'm really at the point where I'm afraid I can't take much more. I have put some thought into taking the children and going to the United States for the summer, like most of the American wives. The thing is I really do want to be here. I want to keep working on my Norwegian lessons and I want Ellen to keep playing with her friends in the neighborhood. She's just getting going here. And even though I really don't appreciate my husband just now, I still love him, and want to be near him.

School is winding down and with that many of the expats I know are going back to wherever they come from for the summer. Many people will be gone two months or more.

But I've got to forget about everything I don't like that's going on right now. Including the recent airline strike that has put an end to my mail, and the bus strike that has forced George into the decision to buy another car and all the other stuff. I also have to give George some space, a whole lot of it, so he can deal with his deal, which I suspect is really getting it together with how things happen at work, the cultural differences there, which must certainly be worse than the cultural differences out shopping.

You know, for comparison I was talking with a Norwegian friend of mine who has lived in the United States and I told her how miserable I've been and I asked her what she didn't like about living in America. Here's what she said: She had to work until 6:00 p.m. every night instead of 3:30 p.m., and that by the time she had been to the daycare, made and eaten the family dinner and cleaned up she was exhausted but still had to do laundry, vacuum, etc., etc.

It is true that while the Norwegian workday is much shorter than we're used to, it does provide a very good quality of life. Day care isn't even open after 4:00 p.m. in this country.

She also said she hated it that she had to get in the car whenever she wanted to go anywhere (she lived in the suburbs), and that there wasn't a playground within walking distance of her house.

There are half a dozen nice playgrounds around mine, and I can walk to the grocery store. These things are very nice, in fact, and really contribute to a good quality of life.

Still furthermore, she said that wherever she went in the United States, but especially when she was in a big city, she was afraid and she worried for her and her family's safety. That is a big deal, isn't it? I remember feeling that way when I first started living alone in Chicago. Turning a corner and realizing that things didn't look so good, turning back quickly and getting out of there. Worries about safety are serious stuff. They make for very bad quality of life, probably more than anything else does.

When I mull all this over, the really big negatives about living in the United States, I believe it's pretty legitimate stuff, we're just used to it. And the things that are bothering me here seem very minor in comparison.

Friday, June 26

Tuesday was the longest day of the year. It was marked by another public holiday where everything was closed down and nobody went to work. Just to let you know, already this year Norway has had these holidays: New Year's Day, Maundy Thursday, Good Friday, Easter Sunday and Easter Monday, International Labor Day, Ascension Day, Constitution Day, Whit Sunday and Monday, and now Midsummer Night. That's 11 public holiday days off. To me this seems like an awful lot of time away from work, but there won't be another holiday until Christmas.

Let me tell you about Midsummer Night, also known as Jonsok, because it's actually a pretty good holiday. We've watched the days get longer and longer and longer and longer. When we arrived on March 1 the sun was setting around 7:00 p.m. The days have gotten a bit longer by a few minutes each day, and now, the sky doesn't really get dark until nearly midnight. And when it does get dark it doesn't get really dark, it's more like twilight. The sky is light again a little after three in the morning, and the birds start singing.

The neighbors all get together to celebrate the longest day by having a big cookout and bonfire. Actually this holiday reminds me a lot of our Fourth of July because it combines these things: casual atmosphere, neighbors, grills, food, drink, fire. Our neighbors were very kind to make sure we knew about the party and several of them went out of their way to encourage us to come out. It was very nice of them and we had a really good time with everyone.

The evening started in one of the large play parks in the neighborhood. We all gathered at 6:00 p.m. and brought our own grills and food and wine. We chatted and ate together. It was a nice chance for us to meet some neighbors and to get to know others we had already met a bit better. One neighbor works for one of the car rental companies and he said my thing with the mirror on the rental car was not at all unusual and that people often rent a manual car, drive it around for a couple days and trade it in for an automatic.

Anyway around 9:00 p.m. we took our things home and met again on Stokkavatnet for a huge bonfire. Norwegians spend the whole year collecting things to burn on the Midsummer Night bonfire, everything from old wooden doors and window frames to unwanted furniture and tree trimmings. And some of the unwanted stuff is not in bad shape. I told one of my neighbors there were a few things I would have taken off the pile if I'd been in my own country, not afraid of neighbors saying something like, "That crazy American was taking garbage off the Jonsok pile."

So they piled up all this stuff into an immense heap and the blaze was tremendous.

Being around all my neighbors reminded me of my need to work hard with my Norwegian. And I still find Norwegian names a bit difficult, but I'm getting better with them. Let me just rattle off the names of some Norwegians I've met so you get what I mean: Ragne, Olaf, Ragnhild, Kristian, Magnus, Kjerstin, Leif Arne, Lars, Hadle, Wenche, Gro, Eli, Svein, Henrik, Silje, Ingunn, Hampus, Ida, Kjell, Gro-Nina, Kjetil, Malthe, Kjellaug, Knut, Hermann, Izak, Bente, Bodil, Tone, Gunn. Bear in mind these are just the names I understand and remember. Do they seem weird to you too?

And now the longest day has come and gone and the days will begin to grow shorter and shorter. My friends say you really notice it by fall, and around November people already will be complaining about how early it gets dark. But it won't be until around Christmas that we experience the shortest day of the year.

And the weather lately has improved. It's been fairly dry with temperatures in the mid- to upper-sixties and we've enjoyed a few beach days. The kids are just crazy when they get outside and they are happy to swim in the icy waters. Many kids don't bother with bathing suits and just swim either naked or in their underwear. Well, adults do too. This is new to us. Then they get out and as quickly as possible they put their dry clothes back on while shivering like crazy. I am surprised by some of the things I'm comfortable with letting the kids do. Not only are Ellen and Peter happy to get all wet in the cold water, then stay out in the cold, they also get really, really filthy dirty.

Ellen is always swinging from a tree or jumping off a big rock and Peter is crawling everywhere over all sorts of terrain. They frequently get in the way of people on the path around Stokkavatnet but there haven't been any problems. Everybody seems to have a lot of tolerance for this sort of thing. Just last night I was talking to a neighbor in the street and our kids were right in the middle of it. Peter is one and Magnus is two. A car came up and we took our time going over to get the kids out of the street. The driver of the car just smiled at us. Most people seem to expect kids to be in the street and they are very cautious. The lack of rush that irritates me in the shops is what makes being outside so nice.

I am having some trouble with Ellen, though. Now that school is over she seems to have lost some of her confidence with speaking Norwegian. While I do let her go out by herself, she no longer wants to. I also find I'm spending a lot of time coordinating play dates for her with her English-speaking friends. This almost always entails driving someplace far away and it is just a bit inconvenient, and sad, because the neighborhood is so nice, with so many children always out.

And as for the trouble with George. For now we have made a pact to just count our blessings and be good to each other. We're trying to stop talking about negative things and instead we're working on showing our appreciation for each other as much as we can and loving each other more. That which doesn't destroy us will only make us stronger. Am I right?

Sunday, July 5

Today I felt the need for a walk even though there was a hard and blowing rain. If I did this in the United States the neighbors would approach me later and ask if I was crazy or something. But here people do go out in a driving rain and it is not considered deranged behavior, I swear. So I dressed Peter and myself in our rain gear and we headed out. There's that expression here: On Sundays Norwegians walk. Despite the very unpleasant weather, the path around Stokkavatnet was bustling as usual on a Sunday. Everyone was out in the rain gear. Children were playing along the water, not exactly on the beach, because there isn't a beach, but filling buckets and throwing rocks and sticks as if it were the nicest day of the year. The ducks and swans already showed ennui toward all the children eager with bags of bread to toss to them.

But now the wildflowers are really starting to grow, and we bring home bunches and bunches after every time we go out. The house is always full of flowers. Outside everything is blooming. The Queen Ann's lace is taller than I am, and foxgloves and rosehips and thistle and all sorts of lovely things are everywhere. Norway is feeling magical to me again.

And way over here we celebrated the Fourth of July, in the usual fashion yesterday. Our friends Jeff and Darcy invited us to their house, along with many other friends, for a big party. Have you ever celebrated the Fourth when you weren't sweating your brains out in a sundress, or wearing shorts or flip flops, watching a parade, cracking open an ice cold beer to cool you off late at night under a shower of fireworks?

It was in the 40s, with horizontal rain. And they did have a barbeque, despite the weather. And we enjoyed ourselves, despite the obvious.

About a week or so ago we went out with many of the same people who were at Jeff and Darcy's. We ended up at a place called the Armadillo Cigar Bar, upstairs from one of my favorite restaurants, Harry Peppers, a modern Southwestern/Mexican restaurant. It sounds like we've traveled very far and still haven't gone anywhere, doesn't it? Actually, I think Norwegians eat Norwegian food at home, and the restaurants, which are quite good, seem to serve anything but Norwegian food.

So I was up there at the bar demonstrating just how very far I have yet to go with my Norwegian when I realized there was an altercation involving others who were with us, including my husband. It seems our crowd, all English-speaking but a mixture really of American, British and Australian, were the butt of some not-so-friendly jokes. In the end things were OK, but it was the first time I have been around Norwegians who were hostile towards foreigners. Hostile to our faces. We stayed until the hubbub was over, and I know I went home gratefully. I wasn't mad at the Norwegians, either. I can understand how frustrated they might feel with foreigners taking over their town. My feelings seem to be softening a bit.

Thursday, July 16

We've just returned from a very much needed summer vacation. We spent a couple of weeks touring around Denmark. It was a very good time for our family, and especially good for George and me. It provided a break from things in Norway, and we were all good company for each other. It was really just heaven.

We took our car down to the southern tip of Norway, a drive we hadn't taken before, along the beautiful coast, to a town called Kristiansand where there is a very nice zoo. From there we took a ferry to Denmark. We headed south, then across Denmark, spending time in various towns. Six hotels in all, I think. We enjoyed some pretty good weather, traveling a country which seemed very flat by our recent standards, and marveled especially at the fabulous yellow mustard fields, which stood out gloriously against the blue, blue Danish sky.

And when we arrived at home the phone was ringing, it was my sister-in-law Jenifer. After she called my good friend Corrine called, on the same day. It was lovely to hear from friends who care about us, and we're all finally feeling so good and normal. Our neighbors all have welcomed us back too, and it actually is feeling like home, way over here in Norway.

Sunday, July 19

George spent the day fly fishing with a friend, Nick, who is originally from Montana and grew up on the Missouri River. He's a very experienced fisherman and an excellent guide, not to mention a co-conspirator in George's addiction. Between the two of them they say they caught 40 trout. Dinner was delicious.

George spends a considerable amount of time fishing here, and I have read that Norway is a fisherman's paradise. I, myself, have no interest in fishing. My only opinion on fishing is this: You get the time away to fish, you catch something, you cook it for me, and come home happy, please. George also gets away every Wednesday night to sail with a regular group that races around the fjords. He races on our friend Ken's boat, called Balder. I think both hobbies, neither of which I share, have proven to be great ways to take in Norway and all the beauty this country has to offer.

And here, as an aside, is something that recently surprised me. A Norwegian friend here who studied in the United States told me she was positively humiliated using the titles we use to show respect, like Mr., Mrs. or Professor, when she was living in America. That's the culture I'm used to, and it never occurred to me that someone might find using titles humiliating. However, I feel that same kind of humiliation every time I go into a Norwegian's home here and have to take my shoes off. The practice with the shoes is more about practicality than respect, I think, but I still don't like it.

Thursday, July 23

Just a word today about a few things I appreciate and what I'm missing. My Norwegian is still not good enough that I can sit down and leisurely read the Norwegian newspaper, though I do buy it and try to decipher it. Since moving to Norway I've become familiar with the British newspapers, though, and I quite enjoy the Times and the Daily Telegraph. I also read on occasion the International Herald Tribune, which is a fine paper, but for my tastes it's really lacking in features so I do prefer the British papers. The problem is that they focus so much on things going on in Britain!

When I moved here I was so glad to see tennis covered so well on television and I have had the opportunity to view tournaments from Europe that you just can't see in the United States. The problem is the commentary. It's either in Norwegian or German. Obviously I can't follow it. The matches are still good to watch but I really, really, really miss the commentary of John MacEnroe. They don't even talk during the points here, let alone get worked up about them.

I feel better when I know what's up. It helps that we have a post office box in Houston where local mail is collected then forwarded to us. It can't accept packages, but we use it for letters and magazine subscriptions. I am always so happy the days magazines come because at least I can keep up a bit with things in the United States. Time magazine is a fine source of information. Without it I really wouldn't know what's going on back home.

CNN is on here, but the news is only a half-hour and it covers the whole world. What that means is that they end up focusing on one big heavy world-news story, invariably a tragedy. I once saw some people playing soccer with a bloody, real human head on the channel—I swear it's true, they were kicking a head—and unless you want the world's big story, there's just not much else to see.

Every half-hour the channel shows world sports (cricket, motorcycle racing, rugby—who is watching that stuff?), financial news, Asian business news, etc., etc. I don't think the producers realize that there are some English-speaking people out there who would like to see something else. Well, I do like a program called the Art Club, but sometimes I feel like everything in English is geared to businessmen. Businessmen who travel a lot and spend all their spare time thinking about their investments. Hey, what if you're the wife?

At least I can still catch Larry King. Can you believe way over here in Norway you can still keep up with the likes of Kato Kaelin and Roger Clinton? The best of all, though, is when my Vogue comes. I have read that magazine since I was as young as the models in it. Brain candy.

So I guess these are my comfort things, which keep me up to date, remind me of home and help me feel connected way over here in a foreign country. Where would I be without them? Isolated and lonely I believe. I am also so very, very grateful for the telephone. The phone bills are huge but so incredibly worth it to be able to stay in touch with the people who matter so much to me. When things are tricky here I can always get instant relief from the voice of someone I love, no matter how far away they are.

And while I'm at it, I must also mention the Internet. Way back ten years ago when I lived in France there was no Internet. I sent letters and postcards, lived at the post office, called family very occasionally. My contact with the United States was sparse. Now it is so easy to stay in touch with people far away. Modern technology has made it possible to live just about anywhere and still be a part of things, if you want to be.

Sunday, August 2

Our first visitors are here!

Our good friends the Woolers—Simon, Corrine, Rachel and Lewis—new owners of our white cat, Goosey, are here visiting us, taking a break from their holiday in their homeland, England. They have lived all over the world and are now green-card-holding residents of good old America. See? See? It's a great place to live. They even got their green cards.

This has been our first chance to show off our new town, and our friends have really enjoyed themselves. We have taken them to see all the local sights, museums, restaurants, beaches, and they said they are jealous of us. Don't think I ever want anyone to really be jealous, but it helped me a lot because sometimes I'm not so sure we made the right choice. They said, as it's only been five months here, that we will appreciate it more and more as time goes on and even more still after we are gone. I bet they're right.

We also took them to one sight I really should mention because it's so interesting. A few weeks back Christin and Marton took us to see an artistic installation on the beach at Sola by a British artist called Andrew Gormley. The artist made perhaps 100 copies of the iron cast of his body. No, maybe more. Anyway, he then arranged the statues all over the beach and into the water. They start far back off from the water, facing the water, and just his head is above the sand. He progressively raises higher and higher out of the sand, closer and closer towards the water, and by the time he gets to the water he's fully out. He then goes out into the sea. This time there's something going on underneath him so that no matter how far out he goes in the water, the water is always around his legs.

The total effect is pretty fantastic. I read that what he meant by the piece is: What's out there? When we took the Woolers there it was very late in the day. The sky was pink and it was so very windy, the kind of wind that's really distracting. Hard to even talk. Windsurfers were flying in the pink background, behind all the statues, and it was so exciting. The grown ups in our party all wore parkas, but the kids slipped into their bathing suits and took a dip with all those iron men. The air temperature was in the low 50s and the kids were so cold they cried all the way home in the car.

It was also nice to take the Woolers on the Lysefjorden ferry trip. This time we took the car with us on the ferry, and we went past the Pulpit and saw a rock called Kjerag (pronounced kind of she-ROCK), a big round boulder which is caught in the crevice of two larger rocks. It is crazy. From it we watched five BASE jumpers leap to their near death, then pull their parachutes at the last minute. I guess they like to wait until the ferry is below the rock so they have an audience.

Just after that is the end of the fjord. From there you drive this fantastic route through 27 hairpin turns up to the top of the mountain. When you get to the top there's a restaurant with a fantastic view of the fjord below. Then if you drive along the road further it's just like being on the moon. Way up there above the tree line there's nothing but rock, with no sign of life except for the piles of stones the hikers leave behind. Little mounds everywhere which would mark their path except so many people have left rock piles up there it looks like some sort of art. And nothing is growing or green. The wind is howling and it's freezing. It's an empty rock wasteland up there and none of us had ever seen anything like it.

It has been so nice to be able to share everything we've seen and done in Norway with our dear friends. It's been good to be in the company of people we've known a while too. I had really been missing friends, and so had George and Ellen. We have had a lot of laughs and I am looking forward to many, many more visitors in the future.

Evening, Wednesday, August 5, my birthday

The Woolers are gone. I am so glad they came. Friends are such an important part of life and happiness.

And now, even though I sound like a baby, I'll admit I was worried that everybody would forget me today on my birthday. Not since I was a child having parties have I cared so much about my birthday. I'm very far away now though, and I really need to know that I'm still thought of and loved.

But in fact I got so many cards and phone calls and e-mails. I am so thankful to all my friends and family for their good wishes. It has meant so much to me. Thanks everybody. Are you curious? I turned 32.

And I must just mention that my mother and father sent me money so that I might buy myself a beautiful Norwegian wool sweater. I hadn't bought one for myself yet, can you believe it? Not only did I pick out a lovely one, I also wore it all day. It's very sad really. The first week of August and it's just freezing around here.

I called my mom, "I bought a really gorgeous sweater. Thanks for the money."

"Oh good. I'm glad you got something you like."
"Yes, thanks. I'm even wearing it now."
"What? I thought you got a wool sweater."
"I did. It's really freezing though and I'm wearing it now."
"Well it's over 90 F here. How can it be so cold there?"
"Uh. Because it's Norway."
"Right."

Friday, August 14

Summer is really winding down. It has already felt like fall for awhile, and leaves are all over the ground. The expats who left town are trickling back and school starts again on Monday. Looking back on it, it was a cold but pleasant enough summer.

I was invited to, and have really, really enjoyed, coffees with three of my neighbors. First my neighbor Ragne had me over, then Kjerstin and then Eli, and here's what you can expect if you ever are invited to coffee at a Norwegian's home: First of all, Norwegians are tidy as can be and they keep very perfect houses. The coffee is strong, and as I like mine with milk, that's very good. Next, you will always be served waffles. Norwegians don't eat waffles for breakfast, like we do. They are eaten any time of day as a light meal, but most often at around 4:00 p.m.

The waffles are much thinner than we are used to, more like crepes, but almost always with a heart-shaped pattern. They are served cold, which is how people like them, with butter and a fruit jam, usually strawberry. Sometimes they are served with ice cream. I was a bit unsure the first time they were served to me. I just waited and observed and noted what to do. You take the waffle, scoop up some of the jam and maybe butter with a tiny little spoon, and smear it on, then kind of roll the whole thing up, and eat it. No forks. Nothing. They won't pick up a French fry but waffles are finger food. You think I'm kidding.

I'm also very grateful that my neighbors have been so kind to me, and it is my turn to have them over now. I have figured out that Norwegians believe very much in fairness, and that applies to giving something whenever you get something. So when you're a guest you bring something. Well, we always do that in the United States, don't we? You get invited for dinner and you bring wine, maybe flowers. But here you do that all the time, no matter how small the gesture on the other side. If you have a friend's child over they will always bring a little candy or something. Something to make it kind of even.

My neighbor Eli was kind to pop by one day and mention that I had some berries growing in my yard that really needed picking. I said, "Oh really, I don't even know what they are. Are they edible?"

Well they are black currants, and we've had quite a good time with them. Ellen and I picked them one day with Eli and her daughter, Anna Carolina. They came back the next day and I had my Scottish friend Ann over, with her daughter Danielle and her son Sam. We were all very busy picking buckets full of the berries, as I have many bushes. It was fun, a party nearly, and kind of like Tom Sawyer white washing the fence too.

We all took some home and I made black currant juice and marmalade (they also are excellent with ice cream and a little whipped cream), and with Ann's help we also made some black currant vodka that should be ready for drinking at Christmas.

We've also been picking and eating lots of raspberries since the Woolers were here. Last night I was walking around Stokkavatnet, eating my way around actually, when I suddenly realized I was about a step away from a quiet deer, who was silently watching me. We stared at each other then quick as a flash the deer bounded off. He stopped, looked back at me, then bounded off again into the trees. We've also seen hedgehogs (about as exciting as the first time you see an armadillo in Texas, and easier to spot alive), and the squirrels are quite red with the big ears just like in Squirrel Nutkin. I've also seen either a small rat or a very big mouse.

And I've finally seen one of those huge mushrooms with the red cap and white spots on it. Just the sort of thing you see in childhood stories about trolls and enchanted forests. Yes, I've been warned they are very poisonous and I won't touch one. Next month, I've been told though, is the time to pick mushrooms in Norway.

Monday, August 31

This morning I am sitting on a patch of moss writing this. It is a fine, warmish day; the sun is lovely sparkling on Stokkavatnet. Sleeping next to me is my new puppy.

His name is Tom. He's a Welsh Terrier and he's nine weeks old. He was waiting for me at the airport, along with George, Ellen and Peter, when I got back from my weekend in Oslo.

Last week my best friend from high school, Andrea, came to visit from San Francisco. She was with her friend Vicki, and they stopped off here for a week after attending the wedding of a friend in Amsterdam. I picked them up, showed them everything, they loved everything, then we all went to Oslo, leaving George and the kids behind.

We caught up with our friends the Villards, whom you may recall we'd met way back at Easter at the Archeology Museum. Last month they moved back to Oslo, where they are from. They told us everything we needed to see and do and they spent some time with us too.

Our trip really started off on the right note. When I was making some arrangements I learned a conference had all the hotels in town booked up. I told my friends we would have to stay in the Oslo suburbs, or else in the biggest suite at the Continental Hotel, a very luxurious hotel right in the center of town. Guess which they picked.

I am very fond of art museums, and we saw Oslo's best, all within walking distance of the hotel, including the National Gallery, the Edvard Munch museum and my very personal favorite, Vigeland Park. We got to the later by walking along the very beautiful residential area that also is home to all the embassies. The day was fine, we took off our sweaters and walked and talked and pointed things out, "Oh, look, there's Brazil."

The National Gallery, as you can probably tell by its name, is the big art museum in Oslo and it houses the largest collection of Norwegian and foreign art in Norway, with special emphasis on the period of National Romanticism. One whole room is dedicated to the art of Edvard Munch, Norway's most famous painter. But if you are interested in his work you can see a spectacular retrospective at the Edvard Munch Museum, also in town.

Do you remember the scene in "Manhattan" where Woody Allen and Diane Keaton are walking and talking about art and Diane Keaton pronounces Van Gogh kind of "Van GAAAH?" Well it turns out "Munch" is really pronounced "Monk." He was Norwegian, after all, and I guess they know how to pronounce his name here. In fact Norwegians think it's so funny we say it, you know, "Munch" like "Crunch & Munch."

Anyway Munch was a contemporary of Paul Gauguin and Vincent van Gogh, in the Expressionist style. His most famous work is certainly the one we call the Scream, which in America is featured in everything from car advertising to blow-up punching bags.

And the Gustav Vigeland park is home to something like 200 sculptures (and his stuff is elsewhere too), which surely must make Vigeland one of the most prolific sculptors of all time. I think his work is so fantastic, featuring people in all stages of life. God surely found a nice place for him in heaven for his inspiring works glorifying humankind.

Though I don't want to sound like a spokesperson for the Office of Tourism, I should mention too that Oslo is home to many other great attractions, including the ski jump and ski museum at Holmenkollen. Someone here told me that if you don't start by the time you are eight years old you'll never be able to be a ski jumper, because by then you will realize how dangerous it really is and you just won't be able to do it.

Of course we took time to eat and drink too, and enjoyed a particularly good meal at a place called Aqua. We ate out one night with Tore and Ingvill, a very enjoyable and memorable evening at Solsiden, and the next day they took me to see where they are building their new home, which incidentally is right behind Vigeland Park. The house they currently occupy belonged to Ingvill's parents, who have retired and moved to a smaller place nearby. Ingvill and Tore will live in the family home until building of their new house is complete, which is on the same property. Then Ingvill's sister and her husband will take over the old house. It's an idea I find so beautiful and it's not the first time I've heard of this in Norway. I know of someone with three generations all living on the same property. Way over here away from all my family the idea seems so very nice.

So that was Oslo, and thanks Andrea for you visit, which again reinforced all my good feelings about this place and our choices. I just realized too that I'm no longer waking up every day and thinking, " Oh my God I live in Norway." I think life may finally be normal again at last.

So what's in store for the rest of the year? I just don't know, but I think life is what you make it. You can either dwell on what you don't like or make the most of what you do like. I need to take some time to figure what I can do here to stay happy, especially as fall approaches and the weather gets really bad. My life has slowed down so much these last years. First was the hectic pace of life in Chicago, a busy career for a big PR agency. Then I quit that and stayed home with my small baby in Chicago while George finished graduate school. Then a move to Houston, where I became ever more domestic and had another baby. Now I'm staying home with two small children in a remote, quiet town. What could possibly be next?

I know, the added responsibility of a new family member. And the dog is so darling. He's my newest friend and I hope he will help keep me from feeling so lonely, because I have been lonely.

Tuesday, September 15

Saturday night George and I celebrated our seventh wedding anniversary at City Bistro, a nice restaurant in town. We looked at each other wide-eyed the whole night. The move has definitely changed the dynamic between us. Sometimes it was absolutely hell being together. Our marriage has been tested. And it's true that things are very different between us now.

I think when you are this isolated from the support of your friends and family and their influence, it forces you together more, as a couple and as a family. George and I will emerge a more grown-up, stronger couple for it. I sure hope so.

It's fall and Ellen has started back up at The Children's House preschool. She is continuing with the same class she joined last Spring, the all-Norwegian-speaking one. She is coming along with her Norwegian, and I really do think it's worth plugging along at it. Our decision to pursue the language has met with some criticism from some of the Americans, who just don't seem to get the point and think it's a waste of time. I've been asked if I thought Ellen would ever use Norwegian again after we leave here. Well I doubt she ever will. The thing is, I think once you've learned a second language, your brain somehow finds it easier to learn more. Plus she will have the benefit of having had a fun full life with the kids in the neighborhood while she's here, and that's worth enough in itself. Research shows, incidentally, that exposure to a foreign language at an early age raises your IQ.

As Peter's just one he doesn't seem to care at all about language differences. He's spoken to often enough in Norwegian and it doesn't even phase him. I have a wonderful regular babysitter, Randi, who spends a lot of time with him. She is Norwegian but she has lived her life in Norway and England and Wales. She is a lovely lady and like a grandmother to Peter. And I love hearing her stories about what Stavanger was like when she was a girl. Quite a different place since they found oil.

I'm going to change subjects quickly here and add how terrifically embarrassed I have been recently to have to engage in so many conversations with Norwegians about the scandal with President Bill Clinton and Monica Lewinsky. You know, when you are in a foreign country people always want to talk to you about America and what goes on there. I've been caught up in conversations like this one,

"So, your President's been a bad boy."

"That's what I've heard."

"I can't believe the American people are talking about throwing him out over an affair. That's so ridiculous! It would never happen here."

"Well, I think there's a little more to it than that."

"Oh, do you mean 'was it really sex,' or the cigar?"

That's just about enough.

Monday, September 21

Ellen is five years old today. Happy birthday darling!

A bit of a rough day, really, with far too many children invited to the party, and some of them dropped off by parents whom I don't think realized our Norwegian is, well, limited.

But let me bring that up for a minute, the language thing. There was a book published in the 1950s by Eugene Burdick and William Lederer called The Ugly American. In it Americans were shown a very unpleasant picture of how they are seen by others when they are outside their country. I have been embarrassed by my fellow Americans here, observing them in shops and restaurants. They are very, very loud, it's true, and they rarely try to speak Norwegian. I know they believe everyone should speak English, and they are irritated by people who don't speak English well. English is not the official language in this country, though, and perhaps they forget that.

Beyond my own observations, I speculate Norwegians would describe us negatively as loud, boastful, and rude. I have been all those things on occasion, since I've been here, and I feel bad about that. The ugly behavior comes on with stress, especially a few months back. But in general I think we also seem to Norwegians to be overly concerned with money, we work too much and we're always in a hurry.

In fairness, I think most people here would say that Americans are very friendly and open. We are easy to talk to, and helpful. We smile a lot, too.

Tuesday, September 29

Do you want to hear something shocking and bizarre? On Saturday, our local newspaper, the Stavanger Aftenblad (which means evening paper, I now know) printed what I would consider exceedingly private information about the financial status of dozens (or was it hundreds) of people around town. My Norwegian teacher brought in a copy of the paper to show the class. I wouldn't look at it.

She said that every year the paper lists the people around town with the highest income, what that income is, what they paid in taxes and how much money they have in the bank.

Can you believe it? It seems like such an invasion of privacy and so wrong, wrong, wrong. And she picked just one name, one that sounded foreign to her, and read it out loud. Well wouldn't you know that name was someone I know, someone I've mentioned in this book. I would not listen. It's just not right. And I'm sure it gives the neighbors plenty to talk about too.

Though I am from and used to a capitalistic society, this is not one. It's socialistic. Recently I've heard it described as Social-Democratic. Whatever you call it, everybody has about the same, or at least they are supposed to and if they don't I don't think they show their money so much with fancy homes, boats, cars and all that. Maybe they do, but if they do, I haven't noticed. You understand the country you're from and the signs, subtle cues and all that. But here you don't need subtle signs and cues because you have the paper.

The thing is big money makes people mad here, because to them it's not fair. And it isn't. As my mother has said to me at least 8,000 times, "Life is not fair."

So true, so true. If I could give part of what I have away so that all Americans could have the same, moderate lifestyle, with no poor, suffering people, I would instantly. I must agree that socialism is a good system.

Certainly here anyway. Everyone is doing fine. I've visited many Norwegians in their homes. They live well. It's very different in the United States. There are lots of very, very poor, neglected people who are suffering alongside people with ridiculously huge sums of money living like kings.

I have no idea what the average American is like. We tend to travel in our own circles and our system is just so different, but I'm used to it so it doesn't shock me. But the more time I spend here the more I think it's a horror against humanity the lives some people are born to in the United States. I lived in Chicago for many years, on the Near North side, not too far from a housing project called Cabrini Green. That's poverty. Or driving along the Katy Freeway in Houston, the homeless are stationed at every exit. I can't imagine what the Norwegians living in the United States think of all that.

In my Norwegian class we spend a lot of time talking about the way things are in Norway in general, and I've learned a lot. Astrid does a good job of picking interesting stuff out of the paper for us, tells us about Norwegian philosophies, cultural differences, simple stuff about food and drink and why it is the way it is. The teacher and the class have made such a difference in my understanding of this country, and appreciation of it.

And here's something that will make you laugh. I was unloading my car after a shopping trip to the grocery store. Unlike everyone from here, I still load up my cart, preferring one big shop every now and then compared to the daily small one the Norwegians seem to prefer. I came out the front door of my house to bring in another load from my car and a police car pulled up. The officer rolled down the car window and asked me to approach the car. They started talking to me in Norwegian and I was so caught off guard by the whole thing.

Not only was it the police, whom I've always found intimidating, but these police were policewomen. And, this was a surprise, they looked as though they had just come from some sort of make-up party or something. They had on so much make-up they looked like they were pretend police officers from a Hollywood movie. And the thing is Norwegian women hardly wear make up. Then they said something to me and I was just standing there, confused.

"Huh? Oh, could you speak to me in English please?"

"Yes. What we're wondering is if that's your purse in the back of the car."

I look over and there's my station wagon sitting in my driveway with the back hatch open, full of groceries, and my purse sitting there too. I must have left it there when I started unloading the car but I really hadn't even noticed. And what did they care, anyway?

"Uh, yes. It's my purse."

"Well we think you should bring it in the house now."

"What?"

"You shouldn't leave your purse out like that. Someone might steal it."

I look up and down my street. Except for these policewomen I don't think I ever see anyone pass the house who isn't at least familiar looking to me, let alone a bad guy. So I say,

"Is there something going on in the neighborhood I should know about?"

"No."

"So you're just here to tell me to put my purse in the house?"

"That's right."

"Thank you."

That is a true story. Can you believe it?

Police officers in most American cities wouldn't have the time to stop for this sort of crime prevention, and it's true that I just don't think or worry about crime any more since I moved to Norway. Why should I?

Several years ago I was robbed while shopping at the Treasure Island grocery store on Wells Street in Chicago. I told the manager because I thought he might like to know what kind of activity was going on in his store.

I said, "Well, I went to take an item off the shelf. These two ladies came at me, one from either side, and it didn't make any sense and all three of us were trying to get the same jar off the shelf. It was all very distracting and confusing and it must have been while this was going on that a third woman took the wallet out of my purse. I noticed only a moment later that my purse was open..."

"Oh honey," the manager said, smiling at my naivety, "That happens here all the time!"

But not here.

Sunday, October 4

If you ever move to an obscure county where people really keep to themselves and you miss talking to people, I have some advice for you: Get a dog.

Our life has gotten so much better since Tom joined our family. Up to now I've been walking on the path by our house, around Stokkavatnet, nearly every day. Nobody ever talked to me. Nobody even looked at me. Sometimes at the kids, but never at me. Now people are actually talking, and I'm getting to use my Norwegian a bit beyond the shops and it's been so pleasant.

Not to say my Norwegian is any good yet. But I have figured out what the questions might be, what the answers are, and I've practiced them. So when people ask how old the dog is, I can say three months. What breed is he? He's a Welsh Terrier. Does he bite? A bit. Can I pet him? Yes, but be careful. He bites a bit. All and all it's working out very well. Also I'm learning that some Norwegians are actually very friendly.

In reality, I spend most of my time with English-speaking people here, but most of them are not American. Probably my closest friend here is a Scottish woman named Ann. She uses the word "brilliant" a lot, but she trills her "r" so much it takes her about a week to say it. She says "aye" for yes and "wee bity" for small. She's a riot and a truly generous and lovely person.

And have I mentioned that I play tennis? I play in a singles league and with a regular doubles group. I doubt I need to clarify that all tennis available here is indoors, but it is good and I have met so many interesting people playing tennis while I've been here. Some of the players are Norwegian. Many are American or British, but I've met Canadian, Irish, Dutch, German, South American, Middle Eastern, Asian, Belgian, French, you name it. They are the most interesting people I've met since I've been in Norway really. Many have lived all over the world, and as many are expats and have been unable to work in the various countries in which they've lived, they have had ample time to work on their tennis games. I don't think some of the ladies realize how good they are either.

The thing is they are a nice, supportive bunch who have more experience than I do in matters of foreign living and they can offer good advice, which I am constantly soliciting. And some of them have been doing the foreign living thing for a long, long time. I've met some who have been doing it 15 years. A very, very interesting life, I'm sure, but probably not for everyone.

And as the weather has gotten pretty bad—wait, it never was ever good, was it—well, as the weather IS bad, I have also begun to work out a bit at a gym. I can bring Peter with me and leave him with a babysitter who works there. It's going OK, I'm able to use my Norwegian there too, and I'm getting out of the cold, wet weather.

I'm learning some new expressions which are exercise-related, and I'm enjoying some of the differences between American and Norwegian gyms. They work out to a lot of ABBA here, and what I would call sort of bad European synthesized music. During the cool down after my spin class (yes, they have spin in Norway too) the instructor darkens the room and actually lights a candle. It's so cozy, as they say here. It is, too.

Cozy, by the way, is a real compliment you can give a Norwegian. If you've been to someone's house and it was nice, warm, comfortable, you be sure to tell them it was "koselig." As the days are getting darker, due to short daylight or just bad weather, candles are being lit everywhere. I was visiting a day care I'm considering for Peter and the little children were eating lunch off porcelain plates by candlelight. The candles, though, and the fire in the hearth, ARE very cozy. They make the dark days much more pleasant. You can't imagine how much you need something bright and warm during this weather. It rains all day, you never need sunglasses and you never, ever have a shadow.

It wasn't until I joined the gym, though, that I was able to figure something out. Even though the days have gotten shorter, and we rarely have sunny skies, people are getting tanner and tanner. Some people are getting so tan they are starting to look like leather. Normal for Florida, maybe, but Norway? Here's their secret: They use those tanning beds at the gym. My gym has eight, I think, and they are constantly buzzing with use. Naked bodies, lying in coffin-like beds, with little lead weights over their eyes, and instead of real sun, just this loud, buzzing purple light. Sometimes there's even a line to get one.

Sunday, October 11

George has been pulled over for an alcohol check, and many of my friends have too. I was starting to feel left out but I finally got stopped at a police check. It was during the afternoon on my drive to pick Ellen up from school. The police wanted to look at my tires. They nearly caused me to be late for school.

The police here certainly play a different role than they do in the United States. Of course they do. There is very little violent crime. Christine's sister is a police officer and she told me that the worst thing they regularly see is domestic situations involving alcoholism.

You certainly don't have to be worried about violent crime like being shot here, or car jacked either. I have talked to a few people who have had their homes robbed, though. I, myself, have been robbed four times, three in the United States, and once in Greece, but the one in Greece was by an American. I have heard from non-expert sources in Norway that the police generally wait to apprehend suspects until they have committed enough robberies to be punished harshly. And generally the thieves' work is done in groups. They watch houses and then when people go out of town they rob them. In my neighborhood everyone seems to know when everybody else is going away and people really do keep an eye on things.

I can't imagine who here would have the motivation to be a criminal. Perhaps it's drunks or drug addicts, though I never see an unsavory person here. Some say there are problems with refugees living here, although I think they end up with a good life after they get settled. Norway forces all residents to learn Norwegian, which is an excellent idea. That way everybody can work. People are always happy when they are working, and everybody who works pulls in a good wage regardless of the job.

That's in contrast to a very common occurrence in the United States, where you have people living in the country for years, unable to speak the language and therefore working in low-paying labor jobs.

On the other side of that, though, is what Norway does for kids living in the country who are from other places. They must still learn the language, so they can go to school. But free-of-charge the country gives them reading and writing lessons in their mother tongue. That's showing a lot of respect for the children, in fact, and where they are from. I learned that a school in Stavanger, called Våland, offers free mother's-tongue classes to foreign students in 25 languages. When I heard that I realized that things can't possibly be as homogenous here as they seem. There are a lot of different nationalities out there. I heard the population of Stavanger is actually about 10 percent foreign.

And speaking of great things this country offers, I have to tell you about what happens here when you work and have children. In the United States I worked before I had children. I worked long hours, had the stress of deadlines and traveled often. Maternity leave offered to me was three months. As I didn't think this was nearly enough time for me to spend with my new baby, and I knew I would have to figure out what to do about the long hours and travel later on, I quit.

Here, when you have a baby you get one year of paid maternity leave. Everybody takes it. In many instances I think the wife takes eleven months, and the husband takes one. It's very good family bonding time. Once you go back to work you can't work the long hours, either, because day care here opens at 7:30 a.m. and closes at 4:00 p.m. for everybody.

I met a Norwegian woman on maternity leave who has a very senior position with an oil company. I asked her if even she could take the full year off. That's a long time to be away from a really important job. She said they had worked something out, and that she works for two weeks and then has two weeks off. Her husband does the same thing on an alternate schedule, and one of them will be home with their child every day. That's pretty amazing, isn't it?

But not as amazing as this: I know an American woman who works for one of the oil companies in the United States as an environmental engineer, and she was offered an excellent position here with that company. Her husband was an environmental engineer, too, but for a U.S. government agency, so he couldn't transfer with his job. They decided that they would move here, the wife would work, and the husband would take care of the children. The problem was that after they'd been here a while the wife discovered she was pregnant.

She had the baby here but the Norwegian working rules didn't apply to her. Here's the great part, though: She was able to take six months off and they let her husband take her place at work for those months! I think that is such a fantastic story and so generous of their company to work that out with them. Now that they've had it both ways, incidentally, they both think working at an office job is easier than being home with the kids.

Thursday, October 22

In the morning the sky has been getting light around 8:30 a.m. or so, and setting a little after 6:00 p.m. Next weekend we will set the clocks back an hour and it will be getting dark at 5:00 p.m. That's really early for October isn't it? The days will be getting shorter and shorter for two more months too.

Incidentally, we had a babysitter recently who is from Iceland, a place that's even darker and colder than here. I put up an ad in my neighborhood grocery store over the summer for babysitters and she was someone who called. When you are a foreigner, it can be hard to find babysitters and you have to do whatever it takes to find them. The church is a good place to start looking, but you're really lucky if you can find someone in your own neighborhood. Anyway, when the young woman told me she was from Iceland, I had to meet her. Up to now the only Icelander I've even known of is Bjork.

The babysitter has been here a couple of times and she is an excellent caregiver, no doubt because she is the oldest of nine and I think perhaps she knows more about children even than me. Why I bring all this up is because of something she said about my glasses, the drinking kind. I have this set of glasses which I've had for some years and which I never really thought about too much. The babysitter saw them and exclaimed, "What are these? They're huge!"

Let me tell you, they aren't. If you've ever ordered iced tea at a restaurant in Houston, well those are huge glasses. These glasses are really pretty normal. But then it occurred to me that I really haven't been using them lately. In fact, the glasses I use are on the shelf below. The ones we used to use only for juice. Those are the ones I reach for now for everything. And I'm realizing it's because this is just not a hot place and you don't get thirsty that much. In Iceland they probably drink out of thimbles. On the other hand, my selection of tea cups, saucers and coffee mugs has expanded.

Then one morning I was heading out with Ellen after my babysitter Randi arrived. I had a cup of coffee in my hand. This perplexed Randi and she asked,

"Where are you going with that coffee? You're not taking that with you in the car, are you?"

"Well yes."

"You're going to have the coffee with you in the car, while you drive?"

"Yes. Why? I do it all the time."

"You do? Why?"

"I don't know."

Come on. Would you ever have this conversation in America? I always make coffee but I don't always get to drink it. Peter and Ellen keep me busy in the morning, so sometimes I don't get to drink it until the drive to school, which is in the next town.

But we Americans always drink something in the car, don't we? Our cars even have built-in cup holders. Starbucks has a whole line of thermos cups for use on the go. I've got several. Sometimes people eat while they drive, though I never do, and I even know people who have television in the car, which comes in handy on long trips especially with kids. Now that I think of it I realize Norwegians don't spend much time in the car at all. They live close to work and family. They often bike or even skate to work, and they aren't slowed down by traffic jams either. In Houston we lived in the car, had good CDs in there. What's the big deal about a beverage or two?

Taking my thoughts a bit further, though, I think Stavanger is probably some many years behind the United States in terms of being modern. I don't mean that in a bad way. Being more modern isn't better, but it is different. And probably unavoidable.

But for now, people here don't have long commutes in heavy traffic. They don't need stores to be open long hours because they don't work late. Few things are open on weekends. Some public places close down for the summer. In all things are just much, much simpler around here.

Here you're either at work, briefly shopping, out in nature, playing a sport, or just at home doing something extremely industrious like building your own addition. People do a lot of things themselves here, because labor is so incredibly expensive, but I think I already covered that!

Friday, October 23

Ellen has been learning about Greenland this week in school. It's part of a project they have been working on since the beginning of the year. They are going around the world with the alphabet, one letter per week, one country per letter, starting with "A."

When they started, Australia was the featured country. One of the children in the class, Conor, had just returned from there. He brought all kinds of things from his trip to show the class. Next came "B," and one girl in the class actually is from Brazil and she was able to tell everyone all about it. With "C" they were in Canada, and there is in fact a Canadian child in the class. His mom came and made pancakes with Canadian maple syrup, so now everybody loves Canada.

The next week the featured country was Denmark. Ellen's best friend Danielle talked about that country, with help from her dad, who is Danish. On to "E" and of course there is someone in the class from England. I'm not sure what they did, but for "F" they built the Eiffel Tower and one of the moms taught the children the words to *Frere Jacques*. This week they have been talking about Greenland. No one in the class is actually from Greenland, but one boy has sled dogs from there.

So he got to bring one of his dogs to school and I guess the kids were delighted. As I understand it, the dogs have a way of coping with the very harsh elements in Greenland. They have this super-rich and very strong-smelling oil which keeps them dry and warm. The down side is the dogs kind of stink like crazy. When I picked up Ellen, she and the whole school seemed to smell very, well, doggy, and the teacher explained that they had actually looked at and petted the dog outside. But everyone and everything was kind of stinky because the oil is just that strong. Because the elements are just so harsh. And I believe the kids were able to really understand the conditions in Greenland through that simple lesson.

And when you think about it, they have learned a lot about the world already, and they are just at "G." Not too bad for preschool, is it?

Since I mention that I will tell you about something we are considering which has caused great curiosity and hot debate amongst our friends here. We did try, when we first moved here, to get Ellen into Norwegian day care. As it was an odd time she didn't get in to the one we applied to, and so we enrolled her at the international preschool. Getting into day care here is a bit like winning the lottery. You hope you get a spot, but it's really out of your hands.

I think Ellen is learning a lot of Norwegian in her all-Norwegian class, and I think Ms. Caroline and Siri are outstanding teachers, but the problem is that although she is always spoken to in Norwegian, she can speak back in English if she likes. And about half the kids or more are native English speakers, so when they play, they tend to play together speaking English and don't mingle too much with the Norwegian kids. The teachers try to influence who the children spend time with, but that only works to an extent, and in fact the more English-speaking children Ellen meets, the less interest she has in playing with Norwegians and our Norwegian neighbors. Even though she is young she knows which one is hard work.

But if Ellen were at an all-Norwegian school, she wouldn't have had the option and she would have been fluent by now. And she would be more outgoing about playing with the kids in the neighborhood, instead of less and less interested. It's so sad because there are so very many children her age, and lots of girls too. In general she spends more time in the house with me than she did when we lived in the United States, despite the fact that there are these zillions of kids playing outside all day in the neighborhood and she's allowed to go out whenever she likes. It makes us sad. Her too.

Next year though she will be ready for kindergarten. We have been to the International School here to find out about it. We met with a teacher and got the curriculum for the year. We met with the elementary principal and a counselor. We even met the admitting director. The reason we did all this, is because we're very seriously weighing out sending Ellen to the International School versus our local Norwegian one next year.

We took everything we learned from the International School, which incidentally is huge, with kids from age four to 18, from 30 or more countries, and had it all in mind when we went and talked to the principal and a teacher from Lassa Skolen, our local school, which is small, takes five minutes to walk to and all the neighborhood kids go there. At this point we seem to be favoring the local school because Ellen is isolated here by her language skills, and not as happy as she used to be. As we made a commitment to be here for some years, and possibly even until she's 10, it seems a very worthwhile pursuit to become totally proficient in the language, for her own quality of life and happiness. In short, a year at the local school might be a good option for her.

The problem with the Norwegian school is this: While the first year is soft, pretty similar to what's going on at the International School for kindergarten, it stays soft for all of elementary school. The days are very short, there are no tests, no grades and things generally go slowly. It's a gentle approach to education. In fact, once a week the children spend the entire school day on a nature walk. The International School, in contrast, quickly becomes tougher, with regular tests, grades, and also longer hours and a faster pace too. Norwegians seem to believe that many lessons can be learned from nature, and you always see school children out on walking tours, sniffing flowers, observing leaves, flexing twigs, you get the idea.

Considering the fact that Ellen will at some point need to be in the American system, she is American after all, and we are going back, she needs the exposure the International School would offer, too. So perhaps a year at the local school and then a move to the International School the following year is worth serious consideration.

We're also talking about putting Peter in day care for a few hours each week. I love being with him and he loves Randi, who watches him two mornings a week. He doesn't socialize too much with other kids yet, and he's probably ready to do more than just follow me around all day. In fact we think he's really at an easy age for full foreign-language immersion, so it's all something to think about.

Monday, October 26

We had a few things going on this weekend which gave me cause to ponder. First was a fancy party Conoco threw at the Atlantic Hotel to celebrate their initial public offering of stock. Up until now they have been a privately owned subsidiary of DuPont.

It was quite a lovely party, with lots of drinks, a nice seated dinner, and a confusing but interesting display of ballroom dancing by some professionals who were brought in for the guests' entertainment. Considering that at the last party we went to there were square dancers, I'm getting the impression entertainment is part of the party package here. We got home at 3:00 a.m., very, very late for us, but nothing unusual around here.

What was particularly nice was that I got to catch up with some people I had met but hadn't seen since that ski weekend in Sirdal back in March. We'd just arrived then, but everyone wanted to know what I thought of things now, with nearly eight months under my belt for perspective. One of the men I'd met said they called me "the lost driver," after the story I'd told about getting lost trying to find Ellen's school via some route other than the one originating at my apartment. He was very, very sweet and I spoke to him a little bit in Norwegian, but explained it was going a little slower for me than I'd hoped. I can express myself successfully at times, but I'm no where near conversational.

Another man I talked to wanted to know about my general sense of Norway now. Well it's a slower pace of life than I'm used to. The outdoors are fantastic, especially if you really, really like to be outdoors a whole lot. Stavanger can get boring, however. But I didn't mention any of that. I'm a city girl, right, and I have never lived anywhere else with more natural beauty than there is right here in Norway. I told him that, and he was proud, but also surprised.

"Well, there are plenty of beautiful places in America. I've just been to Denver on a course. It's fantastic. Haven't you been there?"

"Well yes." (There are mountains, but that's about where the comparison would end.) "Did you have much free time while you were there? Did you get to see much in Denver?"

"Not much. I was there for business and our days were very busy with that. I did get up very early, though, to hike in the mountains for a couple of hours each day before things got started."

"WHAT? You hiked for a couple of hours every day before working?"

"Yes."

"What time did you begin working?"

"Eight o'clock."

"YOU'RE SO NORWEGIAN."

And he is.

Then another man brought up some differences between Americans and Norwegians, a regular conversation I find myself in here.

"The difference between Americans and Norwegians is that you are all always so nice and open from the first moment, while Norwegians are quite closed. Americans however only let you get to a point with them and then they don't let you in any further. Norwegians on the other hand are slow to let you in but then there's no limit."

Hmmm. Very interesting. I'll have to think about that.

I've also heard it said that Americans make their children work too hard on serious pursuits and that we don't let our children play and just have fun like they do in Norway. I have two thoughts on that. First, when I lived in Texas I was beginning to think that all that was important to children and their parents was football and cheerleading. Not very serious pursuits at all really. And secondly, these Norwegians have obviously never been to Britain. Children there reach adulthood by age two.

One thing I have noticed on my own, though, is that Norwegians are much more likely to take blame for their own mistakes than Americans are. If we are in a car accident we're more likely to blame our foot slipping off the pedal or the idiot in front of us. I have heard Norwegians say, "I did it, it was a mistake and that's that." You don't hear much talk like that in America. We are much more prone to make excuses. And then to sue people.

A general criticism I hear from expats, which I don't agree with at all, is that Norwegians are bad drivers. This may seem true if you are from a town as small as this one, maybe, but there is no traffic at all here, in my opinion, and therefore there is nothing to complain about. When you're sitting in a taxi boxed in six lanes of traffic and you realize you could walk to your destination faster than you are paying someone to drive you, and suddenly somebody zooms in front of your cab, causing the driver to honk and hit the brakes, and the force of it all causes your head to lurch back and forth very dramatically, well that's bad driving. Sometimes here you will get stuck behind a very slow tractor, though.

So that was the party. Then Saturday night, with very few hours of sleep under our belts but thankfully no hangovers, we took the children to the Halloween carnival at the International School. Norwegians don't celebrate Halloween so we were looking forward to this opportunity to dress up and have some fun. I think I speak for most Americans when I say that some of my fondest childhood memories are from Halloween.

Norwegians have asked me questions about the holiday, does it have any dark significance, is it about adoring witches, putting ghosts on a pedestal, or could it possibly have something to do with satanic worship. Well I tell them all it's just a great holiday without too much meaning at all, just fun for the sake of itself. So, if you think we don't let our kids have fun, well there you go. Put on a mask, run around knocking on doors begging for candy, eat too much of it at once. Maybe when you're grown up you'll put on a costume, drink some alcoholic beverage from a cauldron with dry ice making funny smoke and maybe you'll find an eyeball in your drink.

Ellen went to the party as a darling pink cat and Peter went as Kaptein Sabeltain, a local pirate. The carnival was very well done, well attended and well enjoyed. What it was for the Vaughans, though, was the first time since our arrival here nearly eight months ago to be surrounded by the company of English speakers—mostly Americans—as we were at the International School. And there was nothing around to indicate that we were even in a foreign country. No signs I couldn't figure out. No need to say "unnskkyld" (excuse me), no "takk ska' du ha" (thank you). It was all very familiar yet strange.

Thursday, November 5

Yesterday night we had our first snow and it was a good one, a few inches and nice and wet for packing into snowballs. There's a sign that goes up at the top of the hill in front of our house when there is snow which reads "akebakke," and it means this is now a designated sledding hill, cars are not welcome. At one point I counted 18 kids out in front of the house sledding and they were having so much fun.

Peter and Ellen each have their own super sled, as does everybody else, and all the right gear—excellent snow suits, waterproof mittens, wool socks, waterproof boots, hats—and all of it is really perfect for the weather. If you saw kids dressed like this in Aspen you would think they were spoiled rotten. Every child is equally well kitted out here, though. No bad weather, as they say. Then the kids got together and started to build a giant snowman. They realized, however, that the huge base would work better as a jump and so they rolled it right into the middle of the street and shaped it, then successfully sledded and skied off of it. It was wild and super dangerous and it certainly made the road undrivable.

We were having a dinner guest at 7:00 p.m., our friend Tore, and while I was getting dinner ready some kids started really banging the windows with big snowballs, which were very heavy and wet and despite my double- (or maybe even triple-) glazed windows, I was afraid they might break one. This is the sort of incident I'm really at a loss to handle properly here with my limited language abilities. You loose a certain effect when you go out to yell at the neighbor kids and they can't understand you, plus you're probably making a lot of grammatical mistakes and in the end they just laugh.

I had this happen once as a student in France. Walking home late at night in the dark a thing really whizzed past my head and I turned back and saw an evil looking kid with a huge slingshot dangling from his hand and I realized I'd nearly been killed by a rock. Instantly I started to really yell at the kid. I watched his eyebrows curve down and his face changed as he tried to make sense of what I was saying. It must have been something totally idiotic, because after I stopped yelling at him he just stood there. Then he started to laugh, genuinely, then just disappeared into the night. Kids don't try as hard as adults to understand foreigners.

But luckily for us Tore was there, and he and George came up with a plan to sneak up and corner the kids with the snowballs. They each headed out the back of the house into the dark in different directions. They cornered the naughty boys from either side. They scared the heck out of them and it was so hilarious to hear them scream in fright. Even I could understand what the boys were shouting in their own defense, "He did it." "He started it." Etc., etc.

But let's leave the winter wonderland scene for a moment, let me switch topics and tell you about a television show I watched recently on a station we frequently tune into called TV Danmark. The show is called Biker Jens, and it's about a Danish guy who is biking across the United States on a Harley Davidson motorcycle. The guy looks like a typical American Harley rider in that he's huge, resplendent with tattoos, he wears a bandana-type thing tied around his head and he's intimidating. Although the show is in Danish, I can pick some of it out and whenever he talks to anyone he meets it's of course in English, though his Danish accent can be tricky to make out. When he offers his commentary, the meat of what he's observing, where he looks directly into the camera, well he does lose me because then it's Danish. But I think I've got a pretty good general feel for what's going on.

I watched an episode where he tooled into New Orleans and his first stop was with a Voodoo Queen. She seemed to sense that he was not taking her too seriously and might even be mocking her, so she played it cool and I doubt the show she put on was anything like what she really does with her clients, whatever that may be. And not that I'm endorsing Voodooism. Anyway, maybe it was her; maybe it was the editing, but somehow though she came across as without any merit, a charlatan. Next he visited some cheesy tourist shops in pursuit of some beads, and then he and his cameraman went around taping women flashing their bare breasts for his beads. Not good. I happen to be very fond of the city, but I have never enjoyed it from the perspective he did. I like the restaurants, the music, the architecture, the antique shops.

Anyway, they showed him next suffering with what I assumed was a huge hangover, and then he hit Whisky River for some burgers, music and a quickie in what his partner called her "Pervertible," which she thought was a funny spoof on what she does in her convertible.

The poor woman was a forty-something drunk who very blatantly picked up Biker Jens, who incidentally does have a certain appeal. To my astonishment he went along with her. She was spilling her drink while driving drunk and made some comment about how you can do that in the United States, plus she knows the authorities anyway. I have no idea what he said when talked to the camera the next time. He had just gotten out of the Pervertible and he had a guilty, sheepish expression on his face.

What's my point? Well his actions were certainly horrible, but he also made the United States look really, really bad.

You know, people doing whatever it is they are doing in America, on TV, in the Oval Office, on the sports field, I doubt they realize it, but a lot of that information makes its way out of the country. Do you think when the cast of Friends is taping the show, a show which is hugely popular here, by the way, do you think they ever wonder how their performances will affect the way people living on the other side of the planet might perceive Americans? Do you think the moguls in Hollywood put even one moment's consideration into the image they might present of the United States through their movies?

But that stuff makes it over here, and it's all that superficial stuff, that sensational stuff, the stuff some people pretend to watch only as a joke, for the entertainment of it. That trashy stuff. Rescue 911 is on here. And Ricky Lake. How do you think a show like that makes us look to foreigners?

And on a final note, I love my country, America. I miss it often. But being away from it has opened my eyes up a bit to things I don't like. I haven't been back to the United States yet, but I do see Americans out and about here. The thing is they can be loud and, yes, even obnoxious. While shopping in a toy store recently an American woman and her son caught my attention. And everyone else's. She was having a non-stop dialogue with her son, saying things like, "Andy, don't touch that! You might break it!" "Andy, what are you looking at that for?" And then the sales person rang up her sale and asked if she could gift-wrap anything. The American said, very loudly, "Are you kidding? I don't have time to stand here while you wrap it!" I was so embarrassed for her. Nobody would have taken notice of her actions had we been in New York. But we were here.

You know, when you are out of your country, you already stand out because you are different. To look at it another way, though, you are kind of an ambassador for your country, and you should be aware of your actions and the impressions you leave.

Sunday, November 15

The form of Norwegian which I am learning is called Bokmål (meaning book template), and it is the formal language you'll come across if you read most anything, watch the news on TV or listen to the radio here. It's used by about 80 percent of the population and it's based on the Danish language. The other main form of the language is called Nynorsk (meaning New Norwegian) and it is used by a small percentage of mostly primary school children. It's a new form of the language which draws on, bear with me, I read this, "True Viking Language." It is in fact a language based on rural culture and you will come across it often enough, as Norwegians make an effort to use both forms of the language for official communications.

The law in fact says that exposure must be given to both forms of the language. Before I knew all this I saw a postage stamp, and printed on it was Noreg. The name of this country as I've learned it, in Norwegian, is Norge (pronounced Nor guh). I was shocked that someone could accidentally misprint thousands of stamps with Noreg instead of Norge. Then I asked a Norwegian acquaintance who explained it to me. Noreg is NyNorsk. A fair amount of Norwegian literature is written in Nynorsk, it turns out, by what are called regional authors.

Then there's dialect. People in Oslo speak a form of Norwegian which is closer to Bokmål than the version they speak here in Stavanger and I can understand people from Oslo more easily. Maybe you could compare it to understanding someone from Chicago versus someone from its South Side. One's a little more educated; one's a bit more colorful.

But let me elucidate a bit more. Before airplanes and helicopters and other modern transport, people traveled little outside their hometowns. The terrain's just too difficult to traverse. In fact you really can't get too far, too efficiently, with a car here even today, even with big tunnels and an impressive ferry system. But people were much more isolated before, and that's where the widely varying dialects come in. Let me give you some examples to illustrate what I mean.

In Stavanger, for example, people say things in the past tense that are occurring right now, in real time. Someone might open a gift and say, "That was nice," instead of "That is nice." This is just a weird quirk in the language they have here. I don't think they use the past tense in this same way next door over in Sandnes.

And the word for "I" is "jeg," pronounced like YIGH (rhymes with high). In Stavanger dialect it's "eg" and sounds like EGG. I hope you agree YIGH and EGG sound very different.

I've learned "Hva heter du?" for "What's your name?" But what people actually say in Stavanger is "Ka hette du?"

"Hvordan har du det?" means "How are you?", but if you are from around here you might say, "Kossen har du det?"

I say "ikke" pronounced ICK AH, for "not," while my daughter, who speaks in dialect, says something that sounds more like ISH AH.

In the end there's quite a difference between the way I've been taught to say things and the way people here really speak the language. I just partic-ipated in another dugnad, one of those neighborhood clean ups, and I went home frustrated that I couldn't understand what my neighbors were saying to each other around me. Very disappointing after all the hours I've spent in my Norwegian class and doing my homework. It's easy to get downhearted by all this but at least now I know it's all that dialect.

I am getting better at communicating, especially if it's one-on-one with good eye contact and someone kindly speaking very slowly to me. That's usually how it goes with the nice dog owners I meet when I'm out walking Tom, but unfortunately that pretty much rules out all good conversation with children. The conversations with the dog owners really encourage me though. I'll chat with them a bit then they always tell me about so-and-so they know, who has lived in Norway for eight years and still doesn't speak any Norwegian. One older man told me he was stationed in Germany after WWII and that he was the only Norwegian in his group to learn German, that it made his stay more pleasant because he could talk to locals, read announcements, and that's the sort of thing I really like to hear. I think speaking the language just makes the experience so much better and more complete.

And recently some Norwegian friends of mine were playfully testing my language abilities. They teased, "Do you understand us better if we speak Norwegian with a heavy American accent?" I really did.

Monday, December 7

We usually leave for school at 9:00 a.m. and the sun's lightened the sky already a bit but it's the moon that's really dominant in the sky. This week I drove Ellen for a field trip at 8:15 a.m. and was surprised to see just how dark it is when the local kids walk to school. It's exactly like walking at midnight. And with the rain coming down and the glare from the car lights it makes it very hard to see those little people.

When we first arrived here we found a small reflective disk on the ground. It was about the size of a lid from a jar of mustard. It was dangling from a string and we couldn't figure out what it was.

They call them "refleks," and they are attached to clothes, strollers, backpacks, pets, anything. When you walk they dangle and spin on the string. Car lights catch them and reflect the light, and this makes you much safer walking around in the darkness. Plenty of people, children and adults, regularly wear full reflective vests for safety too. And the sky is fairly dark from about 4:00 p.m. until after 8:30 a.m. just now. We've still got a couple more weeks where the days will be growing shorter. I met someone who grew up pretty far north of here, above the Artic Circle, and he says that for weeks there isn't any sunlight at all up there. None.

The refleks help, the candles help, the fires in the fireplace help, the gym helps, bright colors in the house help, but the bottom line is that it is not pleasant to be some place that is this dark. Even during the seven or so hours that there is some relative light, like dusk, it's often overcast, raining or snowing. It is quite normal to have gale-force winds to go with the precipitation, too. And when there is sun, the light hardly makes it above the rooftops of the houses in the neighborhood. The angle of the light is so bizarre and it really illuminates dust particles in the air. Sort of like the light coming from a movie projector does.

We have been busy planning for Christmas and getting very excited about that. We always put up our Christmas tree in early December, then take it down a few days after Christmas. Here they don't put the tree up until Christmas Eve, and it stays up until mid-January. I like putting the tree up when we do. When you entertain before Christmas you can have the added coziness of the decorated tree, and besides, when Christmas day has come and gone I'm ready to be done with Christmas and get on with things. I don't want a tree around for long after the holiday is over.

The gifts for all our American friends and family were mailed a month ago. I had so much to send I did it really early so I could send it all economy class. I bought a number of Norwegian gifts at a shop in town called Husfleiden, and at a craft bazaar sponsored by the Petroleum Wives Club. I should tell you a thing or two about the PWC, since I am a member and they have a very big presence here in Stavanger.

The Petroleum Wives Club is a group for expat women whose husbands work in the oil business. The club here has about 200 members. They come from a range of countries though most are native English speakers. They meet once a month, but I've never managed to make it to a meeting. When I first arrived I heard someone call the group the Pet Wives Club, "Pet" being short for Petroleum. I was appalled at the idea of a pet wife, and had no desire to become one while I'm here. However, I think it is in fact a really good thing the group exists. Maybe it helps women the way a sorority helps young women in college. You've got instant friends, an active social life, and lots of support if you need it. My new friend Robin, a Conoco wife and someone I like a lot, is very involved with the group and she keeps inviting me to PWC events. Perhaps I'll go.

The PWC does do a lot to help local groups here, incidentally. Their big good-neighbor activity is the craft fair, which draws thousands of shoppers. All the proceeds benefit local charities. I bought lots of woolen things, hand-knit socks, mittens, hats, and sweaters. I think our friends and family will be happy.

Now we're all just waiting for Christmas, as we don't have too many holiday plans. Quite a change for us. And it's hard to be too excited about Christmas with the other expats, because in addition to the dark outside there is gloom all around stemming from the low, low, low price of oil. It just slipped to below $10 a barrel. Suddenly many people are in fear of losing their jobs, and people whom I thought were really not very happy living here are suddenly desperate to stay. One problem is that people won't necessarily be sent back to the United States to jobs.

And in fact things around the world don't seem too right just now. There's so much going on with President Clinton, will he be tossed from office or will he stay, if he stays will he be effective, and all that. Whenever I catch news of America it concerns the President or layoffs or gun violence; there's chaos in Iran, Russia, Indonesia. Japan is suffering an economic breakdown.

As all the Christmas cards filling our mailbox say, let there be peace on earth!

Tuesday, December 22

Sunday we had Christin, Marton and Malin over for an American Christmas dinner. I served turkey—which didn't taste like what I'm used to but which was just fine—and all the trimmings, as they say. At the advice of a friend I soaked the turkey for a couple days in milk to take out any fishy taste. We also sipped the black currant vodka Ann and I made over the summer and it was tasty.

The tree was of course up, and decorated with our American ornaments which have been a real source of interest for our Norwegian visitors. We bought the tree a couple weeks ago in a rather interesting and special way—off a ship in the harbor. This is in contrast to the tree we bought last year at a big tree farm in Houston. Then we took a hayride out, selected a tree and cut it down ourselves (well, George did). It didn't feel so Christmassy as it was in Houston and we all were in shorts. The Stavanger harbor, on the other hand, was cold and dark but strung with lights and just magical.

Then today I had some of the neighbor ladies and their children over for some Christmas cheer. In Norway it is tradition to bake seven different kinds of cookies and to have them on hand throughout the holiday season for visitors. I reminded my guests that I'm American.

I did make some American favorites for them to try, and in all I think everyone had a really, really nice time. I told the neighbors they should feel free to talk amongst themselves in Norwegian, as it's a good way for me to learn. In fact it really is, and how awkward for them it would be to have to speak to each other in English in the event that I overheard their conversation and felt left out. Also, I've noticed some Norwegians are a little conscious about speaking English in front of each other. Perhaps some speak better than others do, and nobody wants to be embarrassed.

And now I'm going to tell you about the Norwegian Julebord (Christmas table). If you have ever looked at a book on Norwegian life and culture you have read about the very special foods that Norwegians prepare for Christmas parties. I have anticipated attending Conoco's Julebord since the day I arrived. Last year George got to sample some of the traditional fare as he was here at Christmas time looking into the job. I heard all about the lutefisk (not that he liked it), and I was ready to try.

But now you hear about big company Julebord parties all over town being cancelled because of the sorry state of affairs with oil prices and probably they would be inappropriate anyway with all the layoffs. And Conoco cancelled its Julebord. I'm secretly very disappointed. I am an outgoing eater and I really like to try new things. I have eaten all kinds of unusual foods, like rabbit, horse, moose, sweetbreads, heart, tripe, even sheep's brain. I think it's really fun to try exotic fare.

So let me tell you anyway what you might find on a Norwegian Julebord table, and next year if you see me around I will tell you what they taste like. Actually I have already sampled a few of these things, because the dishes are popular throughout the Christmas season and I have eaten a few out at restaurants. In fact there's a fun place we visited recently where you can eat traditional fare and afterwards dip your own candles too.

So here they are, things you might find on a Norwegian Julebord, in what I consider to be a relative order of exotic-ness: Smalahove, half a head of a sheep, sliced down the middle so it lays on your plate in profile—apparently it's quite meaty on the cheeks; a lyed fish, called lutefisk; pinnekjøtt, ribs which are dried and very salty from a side of lamb or mutton; reindeer steak; specially prepared hams; a variety of sausages. Side dishes include sour cabbage and other vegetables, and fruits like cloudberries, served with whipped cream. Beer is usually served, along with aquavit, the only spirit produced in Norway. It is made of potatoes and caraway and other spices, and before it is bottled it travels around the world in an oak cask.

And that's what's going on with Christmas. I confess that I am missing my friends and especially my family over in America. I love them, and my country, more than ever.

Friday, January 1, 1999

Happy New Year!

Well Christmas came and Santa somehow managed to find us. He left lots of presents under the tree even though we had a fire going in the fireplace all day and night on Christmas Eve. We assured Ellen that Santa would want it that way, that we should be warm, and she suggested he might just try the front door.

We had a nice day, opened the gifts Christmas morning—so fun with little kids—and felt like a real family even though it was just us. That night, after the kids went to bed we took down the tree and finished packing. The morning after Christmas, known as Boxing Day in Britain, we were in London.

We spent a week in a hotel on Hyde Park. It was fantastic being in a huge city again. Stavanger is, in the end, a pretty small town. In London there were so many different kinds of people to look at, choices of food, shopping, museums, even a show—just so much more of everything to take in.

The interesting thing was that this was the first time in nearly a year we've been in a country where the primary language is English. It was so very, very easy and nice to be able to just talk to people and be spoken to and everybody understood us and vice versa. I was absolutely sure everyone got more than the gist of what I was saying. I felt competent to really compliment, and once criticize—things I really can't do properly in Norwegian yet. Sometimes I just want to say to someone, "Thank you so much. You have been so amazingly kind and helpful and I sure do appreciate it." Here in Norway I have to rely more on my face, raised eyebrows, humble expression, to really communicate all that.

And you can't imagine what a relief it was in London to be able to walk up to the counter in a shop and simply pay for something without any stress involved. I hadn't realized it here, but when I was in London, just before I would approach someone I would feel a little twinge of anxiety, which surprised me. Then I remembered I would be speaking English the whole time. I must get better with my Norwegian so that feeling can go away.

We rode the Tube and it was easy because we could read the travel information straightaway, as they say over there. No guessing about it. We went into the Natural History Museum and simply marveled that we were able to read the information listed on all of the displays. And George and I kept remarking to each other how terrifically friendly Londoners are.

We haven't traveled as much since we've been here as other expats we know. The reason is because we have a one-year-old child. The trip to London was easier with Peter than our holiday in Denmark, but to be perfectly honest it wasn't that easy either. Babies adore a routine. Luckily we have loads of family scheduled to visit us in the spring, but I do hope next year we'll travel a bit more.

So we left London and headed back to Norway with a certain feeling of dread, and the skies were dark black and rainy when our plane landed late this afternoon. Christmas is over. It's New Year's Day. My resolution is to work harder on my Norwegian and use it more. And to use profanity less. Things with George are good and I'm going to work hard to keep them that way, too.

Thursday, January 14

I wish I were a bear. I would crawl into a cave, pull a rock in front of it and sleep away the rest of the winter. Not that I haven't been sleeping away the winter. I have been. It's hard not to feel really tired and ready for bed as soon as dinner is over. Ellen is totally confused about when during the day it is. She'll say,

"Is it night yet?"

"No, honey, it's the afternoon."

"How can you tell?"

"Because I'm wearing a watch."

But to be fair the days are already longer than they were a couple of weeks ago. They are increasing at the rate of three minutes a day, which may not sound like much, but in another 10 days we will have 30 minutes more of daylight. When we moved here back on March 1 the sky was still light until 7:00 p.m. That's only six weeks away.

Norwegian skies are really unlike any I've seen. In spring and fall we have so many rainbows, and often enough one rainbow inside another. Winter is dominated by the moon, large and low. And in summer, of course, there's more sun than you know what to do with. The mountains all around glow a fantastic purple late in the day. But all the rain and overcast skies make a very gray, dismal backdrop to life here too much of the time.

I seem to recall being very surprised by the change in the weather when we moved from Chicago to Houston. We were so hot and sweaty and tired when we first got to Houston. It was springtime when we were looking for a house and I kept telling my realtor, "Good grief it's hot here."

She, along with everyone else we met, would say, "Oh, this is nothing, honey. Wait until summer."

I only looked at homes with pools, because of this, really a good thing, because we lived in our pool and entertained kids and even adults in it regularly. By the second year, though, we found ourselves saying things like, "It's really not so bad in the shade."

Chicago winters are definitely colder than the one we are experiencing now, here, in the south of Norway, tempered by the Gulf Stream. Again, it's all relative. It just feels so cold here, and we never get a break from the wind and precipitation. I'm not sure about the humanistic, environmental, social or political implications, but my life improved dramatically with the purchase of some seal-fur boots, standard issue around here, and now I see why. They are so good.

And except for walks with the dog, and sledding with the kids when there's snow, I'm inside all the time. The gym really helps. The bright walls and drapes and furnishings in my house help. I find myself lighting fires even in the morning in my fireplace and that helps, but I'm not enjoying myself. It's just too bleak and boring. I love the outdoors too, just not this much and where so much outerwear and underwear is involved. I've had to resort to taking the kids to the indoor public pools all the time. I hate indoor public pools.

I'm really homesick, on the phone constantly, writing e-mails, checking for e-mails, listening to really American music, reading my American magazines, because it all reminds me of home. Ski season is on the brink of beginning. Surely that will help.

By the way, my friend Corrine sent me Starbucks coffee for Christmas. It was my favorite present.

Thursday, January 28

Last night we had our regular dinner out with the Conoco wives and the wives were in rare form. Everyone is very nervous because we are about to find out who's out of Norway. It's not my nature to worry. But people were worried, and drinking a bit more than usual and showing their stress on their sleeves.

I've been really relaxed lately. No, that's not quite what I mean. I've been in a coma. The only thing I've gotten worked up about lately was when Tom, our dog, ran out the door just as we were about to take him for a walk. It was dark (of course it was), raining (right) and as he's black and a puppy, I was pretty sure he would be hit by a car and dead within minutes.

George and I took turns running, biking and driving around the neighborhood calling for him, while the other watched the kids. We enlisted help from anyone we saw walking by. I asked one local girl, about aged 12, if she had seen a stray dog. Let me add that I asked her in Norwegian. "Huh," she said. So I asked again, and again and again. Then with an amazing amount of snootiness, she said in English, "What are you trying to say?" Well it turns out her English accent wasn't perfect. She hadn't seen the dog, either. As she walked away I had this urge to yell down the street, "Don't ever even try to go to the United States. You aren't welcome."

At my next Norwegian class I asked my teacher to critique my Norwegian while I said things like, "Have you seen a dog?" and "Have you seen a small, black dog." She said it all sounded pretty good.

During the missing Tom crisis we called Christin for advice, even though she's quite pregnant, expecting a baby any second. Ever ready to help us, though, she was at our service. She suggested we call the police. This seemed a bit extreme to me, but hey, she's from here. She knows what she's doing. But when she suggested we call I said sheepishly, "Would you?"

So she called the police for us and filed a missing dog report. It was unfortunate Tom had just had his bath, and his collar was on the table, not his neck. But later we did get a call from Falcon, the company that tows cars, operates an ambulance service and, apparently, picks up lost dogs. Some hours after his running out the door, at about midnight, I found myself identifying Tom in a cage at Falcon. In moments like these you don't really think before you speak. I saw Tom and immediately ran to him gasping, "Oh baby!"

The guys working at Falcon gave each other a look over this. The charge for their services, by the way, was $80.

And from that night, until dinner last night, I've been doing a whole lot of nothing. The kids are enjoying sledding, when there's snow. The snow really is great fun, but it usually only lasts a day or so because it's just not that cold (but it feels cold!). I've heard Stokkavatnet freezes and it's a popular spot for skating. So far it hasn't been cold enough. There's ice, just not thick enough. I have taken the kids skating at the local indoor rink. Good grief I'm bored.

Sunday, January 31

Before I moved to Norway it never occurred to me how many people from different cultures I would get to know better by living here. I think I've mentioned that I know people from all over the world here, and that one of my very best friends is a Scottish woman named Ann. She invited us to a celebration of a famous Scottish poet called Robert Burns. We were lucky to be able to go. Last year she invited us to a celebration of Guy Fawkes day and we missed it.

Well Robert Burns lived over 200 years ago, for only about 37 years, and he managed to write numerous poems, songs and letters. His most well known work is the song we sing at midnight on New Years, Auld Lang Syne. His work is characterized as being assessable to everyone, simple, direct. From the heart and best received by the heart. For example, and I'm quoting the invitation here,

"But to see her was to love her, Love but her, and love forever."

There were 200 people at the Burns night we attended, maybe more. The evening started with the sounds of bagpipes. The attire was formal, and men came in beautiful kilts with lovely decorative ornaments, knives, little pouches. The ladies often worked tartan plaid into what they were wearing. Drinking was in order.

Then the haggis, our dinner, was presented. It was wheeled on a cart around the room very somberly. The bagpipes stopped, and an address was made to the haggis. It was ceremoniously stabbed then wheeled away. We thoroughly enjoyed the meal. Next came the toasts, including an address to the lassies and a reply to the ladies. All very amusing, a bit bawdy and set in the spirit of good fun. I recall a few lines from the speech from the lassies. "If you're no good, be good at it." And, "Men are like fires. If left unattended they go out."

The ethnic music was very good, though Ann complained it was Irish, not Scottish, and it was a very dancing, demonstrative crowd. Drinks were splashed around. I watched a man kiss his wife where she bulged from the top of her gown, and someone videotaped it. I went home before it really got colorful, according to Ann. And what a surprise to see so many Scotsmen live in Norway, but it is just across the North Sea, only about an hour's flight away.

I still wish I were an hour's flight from home. Before coming to Norway I envisioned myself with a best friend here. I always have a best friend, and once I make a friend, they are a friend for life. I am still close with my best friend from grade school, Kelly. My closest friend from high school is Andrea, who visited me here. From college my best friend is Kirste, who called us and won the Norwegian sweater. In Chicago there's Emily and Courtney, who we have plans to see next summer. In Houston I sadly said goodbye to Margaret, who helped me with my cat, Barbara and Corrine, who helped me with another cat. I communicate with all of them in one form or another regularly. But I still don't have anyone like any of them here.

I pal around with Ann and Christin often enough. I enjoy them and we are really getting to know each other. As the months go by everything about being here gets easier and easier, too, but some things just take time.

Sunday, February 7

We have just returned from our first hytte weekend.

Conoco owns a number of cabins around this part of Norway. In Norwegian it's called a hytte, two would be hytter. They can really range in amenities, but the main point of them is as a starting point from which to partake in outdoor activities.

Astrid, my Norwegian teacher, has a cabin right by the Pulpit. She just installed running water there. Prior to this in winter they took what she called "snow baths." She said you take your clothes off, run out in the snow, roll around in it, get wet, soap up, and roll around some more in the snow to rinse off. If you think that sounds crazy, I talked to someone here who built a small igloo and lived in it for a week, during her ski vacation.

In a picturesque place called Månafossen, where there's a huge waterfall, I think the water is always ice cold even in summer. We were there hiking in the fall and watched some men come down from the path, pull off their clothes, and jump right in the water naked and shouting in exaltation. Then they dashed out, soaped up, and jumped back in again. Even though nobody in Norway wants to be looked at, these guys didn't seem to mind at all as Ellen and I stared openly, incredulous at them and what they were doing on a very cold day.

But back to the cabin. We went to one on an island called Randøy, a short ferry ride away. The cabin was very nice. Very deluxe really. No need for creative bathing. The weather was cold, wet and constantly raining. The thing about going to a cabin is that there's not much to do besides being outside, because there are few modern conveniences, even if there is a television it probably only gets a channel or two, of something in Norwegian. You can always read. But no matter the weather you go out. And if you have the right clothes, there's no reason you can't enjoy. Once you get out in it, it's not really so bad.

We hiked, George and Ellen fished. Peter found some good shells and Ellen found a dead crab. We had a small boat and putted around in it. We built lots of fires. Played Bingo and War and Go Fish. There was all the time in the world to read to Peter, and there's nothing he prefers to being read to. We went home feeling really refreshed and relaxed.

Since I got to Norway I've listened to people talk about how great it is to go to a cabin. Have you ever found out about something that's been out there all along, but you never tried it. Kind of like the guy in Green Eggs and Ham. Then you try it and all you can think is what an idiot you were not to do it before and that you have to do it again, as soon as you can? Well that's how I feel about the hytte.

Wednesday, February 10

Today Conoco announced re-assignments, early retirements and a few layoffs for their employees here in Norway. It's a sad, sad state of affairs around here and around the whole world for people in the oil business. We wish every family all the best.

All the talk about going back home has made me think about home. This afternoon I called my sister-in-law, Liz. She has just had a baby girl, Caroline, my first niece. I have two nephews, Charles and Isaac. I can't wait to see them and the baby next July when we're in the United States. It seems so far off. That's just a sad fact about living in a country far from your family. You don't get to see them often, and they don't get to see you. We feel badly that our relatives haven't seen our children in so long. We have heard about a camera you can install on top of the computer where you can see the person as they write to you, and vice versa. Maybe this is something to look into.

I talked on the phone a long time while enjoying the day from my terrace. Finally the sun has appeared and the day was really pleasant. The ground was covered in that really fluffy snow, and from my vantage point on top of the hill I could see kids skiing all around the neighborhood. This seems normal to me now.

Christin has also just had a baby, a boy whom they haven't named yet. You have, so Christin and Marton claim, six months to come up with a name for your baby after he or she is born. I found this really strange, even stranger than the vast number of people here who actually have children without ever bothering to get married. It sounds like the stuff of Hollywood to me, but who am I to judge. Anyway Christin and Marton, who incidentally are married, have a new baby, whom I think they call simply "Baby," for now. Christin's yearlong maternity leave has begun—remember, she's been working all this time—and perhaps, I hope, I'll start to see more of her.

Monday, March 1

Probably this isn't the time to be corny, but let me be. It was the best of times. It was the worst of times. That probably sums it up best, and now one year has passed since we arrived in Norway. George and I celebrated with a nice dinner out last night.

What can I tell you to sort of sum things up after a year? Well, it just keeps getting easier and more enjoyable being here, and I'm sure I appreciate being here more now than I did just a few months ago. I don't find people to be rude like I did during my ugly swing on the culture shock cycle, and I no longer feel like the people working in the stores are all idiots. But I still have "good Norway days" and "bad Norway days." In fact Saturday was a little of both, let me explain.

It started Friday night really, when I was taking Tom for a walk and he got antsy then bolted on the leash while I was talking to my friend Marie. His leash somehow got caught around my finger causing me instant pain, but later it got worse. I was up all night with a throbbing finger and thought about just driving myself to the Legevakt, but decided as it was Friday night they might be busy. With what? I don't know.

Saturday morning I was up very early with the thing still throbbing and rang the Legevakt. A nurse there said that a doctor really should look at it, so I went, even though George told me I would regret it. The nurse promised that it's never busy early on a Saturday morning, so I headed in right away. I didn't mind what ended up being a two-and-a-half hour wait, as I knew to expect it and brought all my Norwegian homework with me. I actually had some good, uninterrupted time to do my homework, something I don't get too much of at home. And the wait really wasn't bad. Well, there was an old man in the waiting room—at least I think it was him—with really, really bad gas. But I digress.

So I waited two-and-a-half hours and then I saw the doctor. He looked and my swollen, purple finger and said, "It's probably broken."

"OK. Are you going to take an X-ray?"

"No point really."

"OK. Are you going to wrap it?"

"No. It looks just fine the way you wrapped it."

Here's how I wrapped it: I took a small, cardboard jewelry box and cut the corner off it. I laid my finger on the cotton padding inside, in the corner, so the box protected it on two sides. I held it all together with Scotch tape. So I said, "Come on."

"Well, it might be better if you taped a second finger to it. It will keep the broken one more stable."

"Come on. Wrap it for me please?"

"No."

OK. So I could probably do something better myself. Then I said, "Do you think I can play tennis this week? I have a couple of matches lined up."

"My advice to you, is don't play tennis."

"OK. When do you think I can play again?"

"Don't play tennis until your finger feels better."

"Right."

As fast as you just read that is about as long as I was in with the doctor.

Now you can be sure my finger really was hurting if I took the time to go to the Legevakt, as I had a busy day ahead with the children and we were having friends for dinner that night. So from the Legevakt I headed to the Vinmonopolet to buy wine for dinner. I walked in and took a number. It was 344. An electric sign over the counters displayed the number currently being served: 300.

But two good things came out of the day. At the Vinmonopolet I asked for some recommendations. Remember that you can't actually look at any bottles on the shelf or anything, just that little book thing. I showed the man what I liked, but explained that I was interested in trying something new. He made several suggestions and I made my selections. I paid and as I was leaving he said, "Hey, your Norwegian is really pretty good."

I'm still not at all conversational but I am at the point where I speak Norwegian nearly exclusively when I go out. I even did at the Legevakt. Anyway, I said, "Really? Do you think so?"

"It's better than my English."

Now that made me feel really, really great.

The other good thing about Saturday was our dinner. We had such good conversation with our friends. And are they, a French family of five living in Norway, really so different from our own American family. Not really. What I've figured out is no matter where you are, no matter what language people speak or what they look like or anything else, people are all pretty much the same. Some people are wonderful, others best avoided. But really not so very different after all.

Sometimes cultural differences make it seem like people are really different. The fact that you have to take off your shoes when you go into someone's house, and you're not used to that, or the fact that you have to eat a certain kind of food where you happen to be, because that's what people there eat. If you're not used to a particular accent, for example, or being with people who look really different from you, these things might influence your opinion of them at first.

But I think if you really get to know a person, despite all the obvious differences, color, country, religion, if they are disabled, shoeless, younger than you, older than you, whatever, once you get past that people just really aren't so different. There are nice ones, simple ones, complicated ones, selfish ones, materialistic ones, martyrs, envious people, people with really good values, people with really bad values, thoughtful people, generous people, rats, angels.

I am absolutely certain that when I'm an old lady looking back at this time I will remember it warmly and fondly. George and I can reminisce about it all, just like we reminisce about our days at school and when the kids were younger. The children will have good memories too, of hiking, crabbing, skiing, sledding, their friends, everything they've seen and done.

We have seen so much already, really, and we have only just begun our time here. We are staying another two to four more years.

To be sure we've had lots of problems this year. We all had trouble adjusting. We even talked about going home. But we worked hard, did what we felt was right, and in the end we really like Norway. We have a very good life here. And why shouldn't we? This is a magical place, an old-fashioned place in time that's probably nearly gone from the United States. It's definitely gone from any place we've ever lived. Here's some place where nothing is open so you have to go out for a walk. And there are a million mountains to climb, waterfalls to see, fjords to travel, fish to catch, berries and mushrooms to pick, to eat, and there really may even be a troll out there somewhere.

Just last night as I went around Stokkavatnet with the dog, I had to stop, to marvel at the scene around me. The clear night glowed with stars scattered across an electric indigo sky, the colors and patterns were reflected on the lake, flat like a mirror. On the hill in the distance the lights of the small city were twinkling and illuminating it all was a giant, white moon. It seemed to be up there just for the pleasure of Tom and me alone. And I whispered to the dog, "This place is fantastic."

And wouldn't that be a lovely way to end our story of one year in Norway. But the ending's not quite right. It's just a bit too perfect. Let me finish with this final thought: We hate the weather.

AFTERWORD

Tips for a successful foreign experience

1. Start with a great attitude. A foreign move should be something everyone is excited about. If you are single, you've only got to worry about
   you. Make sure, though, the whole family is anticipating the experience
   as eagerly as you are. If everyone isn't, you might need to reconsider.

2. You get out of it what you put into it. Make a good effort to find out
   as much as you can about where you are going before you go. Check
   out what's available at the library, go online, read travel books, talk to
   people who have been there. It's nice to find out who the country's
   heroes are, scientifically, artistically, politically, and learn something
   about them. Read some history about the place you are moving to.
   Listen to music from the country; look at art books, read local literature. The more you know about a place, the more you'll appreciate
   and enjoy it. And don't forget to be a tourist. As soon as you arrive
   start visiting the sites, and take lots of pictures.

3. When you first arrive in the new country, remember that the temporary situations are temporary. It's hard getting started. It just is. But
   remind yourself that the difficult early time will pass, and that you will
   eventually feel at home in your new surroundings.

4. Allow yourself to be human, laugh at your mistakes and forgive yourself. Moving to a foreign place is such a stress, and it will show on
   occasion. You can count on it. You'll lose your patience and you'll
   make a fool of yourself. It's guaranteed. Have a sense of humor about

it all and give yourself a break. Think of what funny stories you will be able to tell someone down the line.

5. Befriend a local. People who are from the country you are moving to are a great resource—even better than other expats who have learned the ropes long before your arrival. Certainly the expats can help you get started and give you good advice about schools, banks, everyday things. In time, maybe about six months, you'll be an expert on all that yourself. But it will be the local people you will continue to rely on throughout your stay. They will help you to learn about the country, to keep abreast of local activities and issues—and they know about all the interesting places tourists don't. It's also important to befriend local people if the language in your new country is new to you. The other expats really can't give you great detail about a strike or political situation or a good show coming to town if they can't read the paper.

6. Keep an open mind and integrate. The reason you found a foreign assignment interesting was probably because you wanted to find out about the way other people live. If you move to a country where people eat lots of waffles, herring and brown cheese, don't criticize those things, try them. They must be popular for a reason. Try out the sports or cultural activities the locals like. Your experience will be so much fuller if you can see your new country from a local's eye. You know the saying, "When in Rome..." Well, do.

7. You might not want to read this one, but it's the truth: Learn the language. At least a little. Lots of people, especially Americans, claim to have no aptitude for foreign language. It's possibly fear of trying that's the problem, though, or of sounding foolish. Just give it a shot. Drop out if it becomes a real stress. If you are accompanying someone who is working, and you aren't, you may find you have a lot of free time to fill. Just try. You'll have something in common with everyone else in

your class and you might even make a real friend there. The locals will respect you for attempting to learn their language, your self-esteem will grow as you begin to function more capably and confidently, and your friends back home will be delighted when you show off your new foreign tongue. Plus you'll be able to read signs, the newspaper and follow local news—and you won't feel like such an outsider.

8. Get involved right away and you'll begin making friends right away. If you have school-aged children, you may begin to meet new people as soon as your child begins at the school. Other ways to make friends are through church or synagogue involvement, sports like tennis and golf, gyms, and foreign language classes. Just do it, and don't waste any time getting started.

9. Welcome any new friend who comes your way. The people you meet may be so unlike any friends you've had before, you may think you can't be friends with them. Be open-minded and remember we all need friends and we all need to help each other out.

10. Try to remember that your time in the foreign country is limited. Do everything you want to do and don't put anything off. It might be too late if you wait. Live each day to the fullest and you'll have a lifetime of happy memories.

ABOUT THE AUTHOR

Heidi Vaughan has written extensively for numerous Fortune 500 companies and non-profit organizations, having begun her professional career with Burson-Marsteller in Chicago. Currently she lives with her family in Houston, Texas, and works on special freelance projects whenever she can.

BIBLIOGRAPHY

Further information on expat topics available online

Asiaxpat (www.asiaxpat.com)
An excellent site for expats all over Asia.

Craving Home Online Catalog (www.cravinghome.com)
Online catalog offering food, personal care items, over-the-counter medicine and other products from home.

Direct Moving (www.directmoving.com)
Global relocation portal, offering an extensive range of information for many countries.

Expat Access Partner Site (www.expataccess.com)
Leading online service for international relocation.

Expat Exchange (www.expatexchange.com)
An online expatriate community with useful information and links for expats and repats.

The Expat Expert (www.expatexpert.com)
Robin Pascoe's popular web site informs, advises and offers online support to relocating expatriate spouses and families. Also offers numerous helpful links, and information on related magazines and books.

Expat Moms (www.expat-moms.com)
Excellent site featuring articles and information on expat issues such as parenting, handling depression away from support networks, and online counseling.

Flying With Kids (www.flyingwithkids.com)
Site offering travel advice for families with pre-school aged children.

FOCUS Information Services (www.focus-info.org/)
A non-profit membership organization run by and for international UK residents.

Global Network (www.globalnetwork.co.uk)
Part of the Daily Telegraph newspaper, site features an Expat Living section with information, specialists and hundreds of links to other expatriate web sites.

Outpost Expatriate Information Center (www.outpostexpat.nl)
The site of Outpost, the family services center established by Royal Dutch/Shell, is loaded with useful information.

SPIN—Stavanger Partner Information Network (www.spin.no)
Comprehensive web site containing information on living in Norway, with links to numerous expat-related sites.

www.ingramcontent.com/pod-product-compliance
Lightning Source LLC
Chambersburg PA
CBHW030803180526
45163CB00003B/1144